Cat Tales

Cat Tales

The life and times of cats this century

Grace McHattie

LONGMEADOW
PRESS

First published 1992 by Ebury Press
an imprint of Random House UK Ltd
Random House
20 Vauxhall Bridge Road
London SW1V 2SA

Published by Longmeadow Press , 201 High Ridge Road, Stamford,
CT 06904. All rights reserved. No part of this book may be
reproduced or utilized in any form or by any means, electronic or
mechanical, including photocopying, recording or by any
information storage and retrieval system, without permission in
writing from the Publisher.

Editor: Jane Struthers
Design: Peartree Design Associates
Picture Research: Gabrielle Allen

A catalog record for this book is available
from the Library of Congress.

ISBN 0-681-41570-3

Printed and bound in Great Britain by Butler & Tanner Ltd, Frome

First edition

CONTENTS

INTRODUCTION

MOST OF US know a lot about the modern cat and its life today. We're familiar with the lives cats led in ancient Egypt where they lived like gods and died like kings. And we know of the persecution and the cruelties carried out against the cat during the Middle Ages.

But how much do we understand about the life of the cat in the earlier part of our own century? This mystical creature began the century as a pauper — little more than a misunderstood and sometimes mistreated rat-catcher. As our century ends the cat is prince, poised to take over as the most popular pet on every continent. So what happened in between? After all, in thousands of years

we may have changed dramatically, although the timeless cat has not, no matter how our conception of it has changed.

CATS IN ANCIENT EGYPT

The ancient Egyptians may have been the first to appreciate the skills of the cat. In their inhospitable climate, harvested grain was precious and irreplaceable, so any creature that helped to protect it was treated well. The cat was a deity in ancient Egypt and a most valuable creature because it not only offered friendship and love to humans but it also

Detail from an ancient Egyptian tomb painting.

killed rats and mice and was a companion in hunting. Early wall paintings show cats retrieving birds shot down by bow and arrow.

Little wonder, then, that they were cared for as miniature humans and particularly favoured cats were bedecked with earrings and necklaces. During a fire, Egyptians were more concerned about saving their cats than putting out the blaze in their homes, and owners went into mourning on the death of their cats, shaving their brows as a mark of respect. Cats were mummified and buried with full honours in beautifully-worked mummy cases of wood or bronze, some set with eyes of semi-precious stones. Anyone responsible for the death of a cat paid a heavy penalty.

One ancient king of Persia, aware of the high esteem in which the Egyptians held cats, gave each of his soldiers in the front line a cat to carry, knowing that the warring Egyptians would rather give up their fight than risk harming a feline.

THE CAT GROWS UP

In Roman times too, the cat had its place. Several Roman goddesses were associated with cats and the Roman goddess of Liberty was depicted holding a cup in one hand, a broken sceptre in the other and with a cat lying at her feet.

Cats were valued in many cultures for their rat-catching and food-protecting abilities. In Abyssinia, for example, cats were so valuable that a girl who was

An Egyptian going into mourning for the death of her cat.

likely to inherit a cat was considered a great heiress.

By the fifteenth century, cats' fortunes were on a downslide. They would be walled up (often alive) in new buildings to bring good luck to the inhabitants. And in the Middle Ages millions of women – and cats – died together at the stake because cats were believed to be the familiars of witches and witches were thought sometimes to adopt the shape of cats.

In an agricultural economy cats were valuable in keeping down rodents; a skill they took with them to factories and warehouses during the Industrial Revolution. Their skills were equally sought after in the home in the days before powerful rodent poisons were developed.

It is only in the last 30 or 40 years that the cat has no longer been kept in homes as a worker and its status has consequently been elevated. *Cat Tales* sets out to show you how remarkably the life of this most popular of animals has altered during this century.

Roman mosaic from Pompeii.

EXPLANATORY NOTE

Most sums of money mentioned in *Cat Tales* are in pre-decimal sterling currency – pounds, shillings and pence. There were 20 shillings in one pound and 12 pence in one shilling. One guinea was worth one pound and one shilling.

At the rate of exchange current just after the Second World War, one pound equalled four US dollars and a shilling was worth 20 cents.

WORKING CATS

AT THE END of the twentieth century our idea of a working cat is likely to be a pretty, fluffy feline model posing for a chocolate box or languidly stretched out in front of a radiator for a central heating commercial. Earlier this century, however, the working cat really had to work hard for its living as a rat and mouse catcher, a vital role before the advent of the more effective rodent poisons of the 1960s.

RAT-CATCHING CATS

Dr Adrian Loir of Le Havre, France, was the first (and possibly only) person to cultivate a special rat-catching breed of cat from felines which showed those particular skills. In doing so, he was ahead of his time; not only did he appreciate that the kittens of good hunters often became good hunters themselves, but he was at the forefront of the belief that ratting cats should be kept well-fed.

Before that, it was thought that ratters and mousers should just be given milk to drink and should be expected to catch their own solid food. Dr Loir pointed out that ratters were superb athletes and

Peanuts (lying down) was Romford Council's cheapest employee in the 1960s – his wages were just 2 pints (1 litre) of milk and four cans of food a week. These were shared with his 'wife' (left) and their son and subsidized with mice and rabbits.

that rats were dangerous enemies. Like any athletes, he maintained, cats should be fed on the best food available so they would be in the peak of condition in order to perform at their best. Something else that was little understood at the time is that many cats have a physiological reaction to the lactose in milk, resulting in stomach upsets – which is another reason why they were often banished to live out of doors!

CATS IN THE CIVIL SERVICE

Civil Service cats fared better than many others, although there was a definite hierarchy. In the early 1930s, Post Office cats earned from sevenpence to one shilling a week. One poor cat, called Peter, served on HMS *President*, a training ship lying off the Embankment in London. 'In receipt of naval pay' Peter was given one paltry shilling per month, despite repelling all boarders including a cat who tore off Peter's ear.

Cats have been recognized as Civil Servants since the time of Henry VIII when the tradition of having a Treasury cat started. The most famous of them was Rufus, also known as Treasury Bill, who worked in the late 1920s and 1930s and was paid one shilling and sixpence per week. When he died in 1937 he was replaced by Bob and Heather. In October 1940, when the building in which he worked was damaged by enemy action, Bob was taken off the payroll and became a pet in Downing Street. He was

The station cat at Pulborough, Sussex, enjoying a nap.

often to be seen sitting on the steps of the Prime Minister's residence during the Munich crisis. His presence was seen as a good omen. He also became a personal friend of Winston Churchill. Heather met an untimely end in April 1941 while ratting in a storeroom. They were among the last of the Treasury cats as it is no longer considered necessary to employ a feline.

Immediately after the Second World War the Ministry of Transport and Civil Aviation had 16 cats on its payroll. Some London museums also employed cats. In 1936 a case was made out for an official cat at the London Museum on the grounds that 'the cat is an essential colleague, the mice have a special penchant for royal under-linen'!

Mice, it seems, also have a penchant for money — as a snack! Cats were employed for many years by the postal services, who kept them to kill mice which otherwise ate sacks of money orders, costing thousands of pounds each year. The cats started off by earning sevenpence a week for their food and milk, rising in cases 'where exceptional energy, initiative and good judgement are displayed' to one shilling a week.

At this time, a form was sent to all local postmasters. It asked:

Is an official cat still maintained on
  the premises?
Is the authorized weekly allowance
  still claimed?
Is a cat still necessary?

One Post Office official answered question three by writing 'A cat is still necessary and a statement is enclosed showing the number, colour and approximate age of official mice captured in the past twelve months. It is considered that the exceptional energy, initiative and good judgement displayed by this member of staff calls for official recognition and it is recommended that the weekly allowance be increased by twenty per cent.'

In France, qualifications for such jobs were much more stringent. No cat was allowed to take up a government position until it had first served an apprenticeship on a warship where the rats were much larger and harder to catch. It was then promoted from the Navy to a much easier Civil Service position.

There was provision in the French Budget for 13 official cats – 12 worked for the Foreign Office and one in the National Library. As the Library was so large, that cat was paid the French equivalent of three shillings and ninepence per month while the other 12 cats had a mere seven shillings and sixpence per month to share between themselves.

Wages for cats gradually rose over the years, but today, cats in government departments are not officially on a payroll and live on gifts from their Civil Service colleagues.

SHIPS' CATS

Cats were very popular (and still are) on ships. Many people have attributed this to a need of the bluffest of sailors to nurture and care for small creatures. The truth may be less philanthropic.

A great deal of superstition has always surrounded the ships' cat. In Victorian times it was believed that a sailor who owned a black cat would never drown, which led to such a huge demand in coastal areas for black cats that they had to be kept under lock and key for fear of

theft. Cats with more than the usual 18 toes were also considered lucky, as were tortoiseshell cats in some areas.

In fact, ships' cats were encouraged by the owners more than the sailors, because marine insurance didn't cover damage to cargo from rats. If the owner of the cargo could prove that no cat was carried on board, he could claim compensation from the ship's owner. For the ship's owner, it was much easier and cheaper to have a cat on board.

The cat performed another vital function, concerned with the marine law of salvage. Cats, being territorial creatures, never wanted to leave their floating homes even when they were sinking, so often they were the last creatures left on board after a disaster of any sort. Under the law of salvage, any ship

Fleet, Air and Arm, mascots adopted by the Fleet Air Arm after their mother was killed near their naval base.

rescuing another which had no living creature aboard was entitled to all salvage rights. The ship was considered a derelict and all property rights were forfeited. However, if anything living was left on board – and this included a cat – the ship remained the property of the original owner.

Of course, this doesn't mean that the sailors working alongside these very important felines were immune to their charms – far from it. History abounds with stories of sailors risking their lives to save their furry companions.

During the Second World War, a sailor called Mr Haslam jumped overboard to save his ship's tortoiseshell cat from a watery grave. Remarkably, it was the second rescue he had carried out in a few hours. Earlier, he had jumped overboard to save the ship's mate.

Cats quickly adjusted to their shipboard life and clambered up rigging like monkeys, lay in pools of water when they wished to cool down and ran along the rails oblivious of the drop beneath them. One day Conrad, the ginger cat of the full-rigged ship *Joseph Conrad*, fell overboard. He immediately began swimming after the ship. The commander hesitated to turn about and risk his ship but, as he watched, an albatross swooped down to attack the swimming cat. Conrad reached up and punched him on the beak. Impressed by the little cat's bravery, the commander ordered a boat to put out to rescue him.

Sidney James didn't even need such human assistance. Ashore in Bootle on Merseyside, he heard the ship's siren and raced back only to find he was too late. His ship had sailed without him to Buenos Aires. When it arrived at its destination, the sailors were much surprised to see Sidney James sitting on the dock waiting for them. He had taken passage in a mail steamer which sailed from Liverpool the same night his ship had left but had arrived six days earlier.

Many ships' cats also saved lives. Lizzie was the mascot of the American Forty Fathoms trawler, *Whitecap*. One day a fire broke out in the galley and swept up to the cabin where the captain, Gus Dunsky, was asleep. Despite having to 'leap through smoke and flame with sparks showering about her, she scratched him awake' and saved his life.

SHOPS' CATS

In the early part of this century, most shops had a resident cat. This worried many cat-lovers because some of the animals were left locked in the shops at weekends with little in the way of food or drink. A member of the Cats Protection League in London visited her local shops before the Christmas holidays and offered to post cat food through each letterbox. She was most impressed that only two shopkeepers took up her offer; all the others either visited their cat daily or took it home with them for the holiday.

Cats are still important members of many shops, although today their role seems to be more concerned with public relations than mouse-catching. Charcoal is one such cat, who lives in the Wells Hardware Store in New Albany, Indiana, and often has customers fighting over his favours. People travel from miles away just to see him, because he's known as the cat who can write his ABCs. A child was in the store with her parents and was practising her ABCs on a piece of paper. The store's owner joked that his cat could write his ABCs too and propped the pen in Charcoal's paws, where the cat allowed it to remain. This is one of the tricks he shows visitors, as well as performing somersaults in the store window. His owner was given a blank cheque from someone wishing to buy Charcoal, but he turned it down.

FARM CATS

Cats have always been very necessary on farms to keep down the rodent population. In 1942, there were an estimated

1,250,000 cats living on farms in the United Kingdom. They were often not treated well, being expected to catch their own food and perhaps given just an occasional bowl of milk. Little wonder, then, that many found their food elsewhere. One travelling fishmonger of the 1930s tells of the four farm cats on his round who would wait outside their gate at 8.30 a.m. on Wednesdays and Fridays for the scraps of food he would throw them. They knew exactly when he was due and would not sit there on any other days or at any other times.

An American farmer in 1947 appreciated how valuable his cat was. He estimated that, far from costing him money, it saved him $805 in loss of grain and destruction to buildings by rodents over its lifetime, or $134 each year.

Messenger boys were sent out to round up all available cats when a top London store was over-run by mice in 1938.

Swan and Edgar were two wartime farm cats who had a very pleasant life. They would sit by their owner's side as she milked her cows, waiting patiently for their share. They even had their favourite cows and enjoyed Buttercup's milk best because it was so creamy, but

would not touch the milk from Daisy, nor would they ever steal from the pans of cream set out in the dairy. Swan and Edgar had their own productivity bonus

A Pears soap advertisement from 1895.

system. A Land Girl who was helping on the farm devised a method of paying the cats for the mice and rats they caught. She would take their tails to the farmer, demanding one penny for a mouse's tail and twopence for a rat's tail. The money

was placed in a tin in the dairy shelf and used to buy treats for the feline workers.

Despite their vital role in keeping down vermin, country cats were often treated like vermin themselves. Game-keepers trying to protect their young pheasants would nail the corpses of animals they had caught to their gates: their employer would pay threepence for each one. It was also thought to act as a warning to other furred and feathered trespassers. Frequently, cats' tails were displayed, but only the tails, so the owners couldn't identify their animals.

OTHER IMPORTANT FELINE JOBS

One American cat has a most important job today. Smudge La Plume sounds more like a burlesque queen than what she really is — the elected mayor of Guffey, Colorado. Her office is in a cardboard box inside a local store, and she's the second feline mayor of the town. Paisley, a calico (tortoiseshell and white) cat was elected in 1988 but died soon after.

Cats have had all sorts of work. In 1941, an advertisement appeared in the *Christ Church Weekly News*.

Vacancy for a smart cat. Congenial work. Frequent outings. Comfortable home. No bad language (clergyman's household). Apply in the first instance to The Mouse Controller, Woburn Square.

COMMUTING CATS

Cats have also worked at railway stations and over 500 cats were kept at the warehouse of British Railways. There are many stories of railway cats, who appear to have been great travellers, boarding a train to the nearest city in the morning and returning in the evening after picking out the correct train from dozens sitting in the station.

A longhaired cat living in Carlisle Citadel Station spent one day travelling to Euston station in London – over 300 miles (120 km) – and the next returning to Carlisle. He never missed the train or got on the wrong one. He also chose the most prestigious and luxurious train of the time – the *Royal Scot*. Sadly, he was run over one day while crossing the tracks at Carlisle.

Station staff became very fond of their cats, as the epitaph on a cat's grave at Goodwick Railway Station shows:

Here lies the dear old station cat.
She killed some mice and many a rat.
Her days are gone, she did her best.
And now in peace she's laid to rest.

Tinker, the station cat of Tiviot Dale Station in Stockport, was the biggest and oldest cat on the railways. He was a champion ratter and caught as many as nine a day. A very careful cat, he always looked up and down the line before crossing to the opposite platform. When he died in 1941, Joe the porter was asked if he had been killed by a train. 'Not on your life, sir,' he replied. 'He just died, and if you want a reason, well, there

Found in 1948 after a 70 mph (112 kph), 158 mile (254 km) journey, underneath a train, this cat was adopted by railway workers and later gave birth to two kittens.

wasn't a rat left on the station to kill. He kind of lost all interest in life after the last rat had gone.' Appropriately, Tinker was buried above his favourite rat-hole.

It wasn't only on the railways that cats were thought to be useful. In 1936 it was seriously suggested that cats should be introduced as regular members of the crew in airliners to kill mice.

TREADING THE BOARDS

An even more glamorous profession was that of the theatre cat. Often hammier than the actors, it was a not uncommon occurrence for the theatre cat to join in the action on stage. One American actor was perplexed when his long dramatic speech was greeted by ever-increasing shrieks of laughter from the audience. He turned around to find the theatre cat sitting behind him, calmly washing its face. 'This is supposed to be a monologue, not a catalogue', he quipped.

The cat at one theatre in the North of England answered to Moggy, Tiddles or Puss, not having a name which anyone knew. After incurring the displeasure of a very grand actress for upstaging her one night, Puss contented himself with mouse-catching and used to line up his considerable haul each night at the front of the stage. One night the theatre put on a new play, in which a mechanical bird on a strong spring was an important prop. After the show, Puss pounced on it, then felt a searing pain in his leg. The spring in the prop had broken his leg and Puss had to wait until the following morning for the theatre staff to return and find him. They took him to a vet and his leg was encased in plaster.

Much to the surprise of the staff when they returned the following morning, two mice were laid out on the stage as if Puss's accident hadn't happened. The following night, two more mice were caught. Mystified as to how a cat with its leg in plaster could catch mice, two of the staff decided to stay behind one night to find out. They hid behind the curtain and watched as the cat hobbled to his position at a mouse hole. When a mouse popped out, the cat hit it over the head with his plaster cast.

Other cats in the spotlight didn't enjoy their work so much. The *Goldwyn Follies of 1938* featured 300 cats which were chased on to the set by an air hose. Many were very frightened and by mid-afternoon all were so tired they stayed

Peter O'Toole – dressed as Queen Elizabeth I – in the 1992 film Rebecca's Daughters, *with a thespian cat.*

where they dropped and wouldn't react to bits of fish used as an enticement in a scene. The cats had been bought from an animal dealer and it was suspected some had been stolen, so after filming they were given away.

By the 1960s, conditions for acting cats had changed somewhat for the better – although not entirely. A cat model in a London studio was to adver-

tise cat food, but was not at all interested in the food it was supposed to be endorsing, so the director added chopped-up

Black cat inspecting a line of auxiliary firemen in 1939.

fish to the bowl. The cat enjoyed that, but insisted on walking to the bowl from the wrong direction. In the end, a piece of transparent thread was attached to the cat and he was dragged across the studio floor to the bowl.

CARING CATS

Guide dogs for the blind are common-place nowadays, as are hearing dogs for the deaf, but few people realize that cats have fulfilled these functions too. Many cats, without training, have appeared to understand that their owners cannot hear and therefore alert them to doorbells or telephones ringing.

A longhaired white cat became the eyes of her blind American owner and would help her navigate around obstacles by warning flicks of the tail.

Even more unusual, an 18 month-old Black Persian called Inky became the eyes of Penny, an Eskimo Spitz dog, after the death of the maid who had cared for her. Although she had never liked the dog, Inky began to take Penny for walks, allowing her to follow close behind and fighting off any dogs that bothered Penny.

FAMOUS FELINES

The world's champion ratter was thought to be Minnie, who killed 12,480 rats during six years at the White City Stadium in London. At the time, the Stadium was used for greyhound racing.

Some modern-day cats still fulfil their traditional roles as mousers. Towser, a tabby and white female cat who worked for the Glenturret Whisky Distillery in

Champion ratter Towser.

---

finest – she was born in the stillhouse of the distillery in 1963, where her mother had been the official mouser before her. She not only killed mice but also rats and any passing pheasants or rabbits.

Crieff, Scotland, had a record-breaking reputation. She is believed to be the greatest mouser who ever lived, having dispatched an estimated 28,899 mice, at a rate of three a day, during a career spanning more than twenty years.

Champion mousers are born and not made and Towser's pedigree was the

Towser had excellent working benefits, including staff lunches in the distillery restaurant where she would eat leftovers of best Scottish smoked salmon and prawns. Her hard-working but rewarding life obviously agreed with her for she lived to be almost 24 years old – 10 years above the average cat's lifespan. In her time she was well-loved, not just by staff but also by the 150,000 tourists who visit the distillery each year. Each Christmas, Towser would receive about 100 Christmas cards from well-wishers all over the world, as well as gifts of money with which to buy her blankets, catnip toys and other luxuries.

When Towser died in 1987, a replacement kitten was given to the distillery by the Royal Society for the Prevention of Cruelty to Animals. Called Mr Toddy, he was so popular with visitors that he was kidnapped the following year and hasn't been seen since. A reward has been offered for his safe return.

Towser's place is now filled by a stray who walked in one day, made herself at home, and gave birth to a litter of kittens. One of them now shares mouse-catching duties with her. Appropriately named, Amber and Nectar now keep the home of the amber nectar vermin-free.

Napoleon of Baltimore was once the most famous cat in the United States and probably had the most unusual job of all – he was a weather forecaster. If he slept

Mr Toddy – gone missing.

on his stomach, rain would soon fall. If he lay on his side, it would be dry. The height of Napoleon's fame came during the drought of 1930 when he lay on his side for weeks on end. Farmers would telephone Napoleon's owner, Mrs Fannie de Shields, to ask if 'that durned cat' was sleeping on his stomach yet.

THE WAY CATS WERE FED

NOWADAYS, FEEDING A CAT is very simple. Yet, surprisingly, the very wide range of prepared foods which are available may mean that the average modern cat is eating a less varied diet than its Victorian predecessors.

SPECIALLY PREPARED MEALS

At the beginning of the century, well-cared-for cats lived mostly on meals prepared specially for them, plus some leftovers. Cat owners were advised to cater specially for their cats if their own meal consisted of something the cats didn't eat or like. If nothing suitable was found in the larder, a lightly-boiled egg was recommended (but not if one lived in London – London eggs could not 'be depended upon').

The suggested diet was remarkably 'human'. Brown bread soaked in warm milk or porridge with milk was served for breakfast; for dinner, there would be 2 oz (50 g) of fresh cooked meat with potatoes and other boiled vegetables, especially greens. A milk pudding (such as custard, blancmange, tapioca or ground rice) was suggested for dessert. Supper was the same as breakfast, with the optional addition of meat or fish. The recommended meats were rabbit, liver, tripe (the stomach lining of sheep) or lights (lungs, which have almost no nutritional value).

Another authority suggested boiling

Pussy's Breakfast

sheeps', rabbits' or cods' heads until the flesh fell off the bone. If the cat's appetite was depressed, it could be enlivened by a fowl's head complete with feathers, given raw. Or owners were advised to shoot or trap a sparrow and feed it freshly-killed, feathers and all, to their pet.

GOURMET CATS

Cats then, as now, had their own preferences. A cat called Victor, renamed Vegetarian Vic, was said to 'despise milk, dislike liver and loathe fish'. He relished cauliflower, Brussels sprouts, potatoes and carrots, but his favourite food by far was fruit. Bananas, figs and dates in particular had to be locked away, otherwise he would eat the lot. Vic had coffee for breakfast, tea in the afternoon and cocoa for supper – all with lots of sugar. He also loved iced cake.

Pre-war cats seem to have been great cake-lovers. At least one cat was said to know the difference between home-made cake, which he adored, and shop-bought cake, which he scorned. His mistress, trying to impress visitors by passing off shop-bought cake as home-made was mortified when her cat sniffed the plate and walked off with his nose in the air.

Tom shared a passion with many other cats of the time – he was partial to beetroot and beetroot tails, while his companion Hester adored cucumber. Another cat enjoyed Heinz tomato soup, a slice of cake, afternoon tea bread and butter, beetroot and thin slices of cheese, all eaten as snacks.

GOOD HOUSEKEEPING

MARCH, 1922   ONE SHILLING

Marie Corelli   William J. Locke   Clemence Dane
Lady Astor   Robert Hichens   Kathleen Norris

A cover cat of 1922.

Some lucky American cats were given catnip tea, made by steeping one table-spoon of dried catnip in a quarter of a cup of boiling water for two minutes. This was then strained and two table-spoons of the liquid poured into a saucer of cream.

Most cats were still given milk, and milk puddings were particularly popular. A grey Persian called Trotsky enjoyed milk puddings but his favourite meal was baked beans 'in spite of audible discomfort 20 minutes later'. He can hardly have been a pleasure to be with as he also ate boiled onions, as well as tomato soup, blackcurrants and gooseberries.

THE RAW MEAT DIET

By the 1930s, Arthur M Turner, a man with 40 years of cat-keeping experience, believed that the main diet of the short-coated domestic feline should be raw meat and water. When the cat was six years old, a little ox liver could be added to the diet. Of their longhaired cousins he said, with a note of exasperation, 'Fluffy cats... are, or have been, so artificially bred that they seldom take to a natural diet. Some of them will eat almost anything.' At weekends Mr Turner fed his cats raw and stewed rabbit but noted that his cats preferred it raw (not recommended today for fear of salmonella poisoning).

He also suggested rabbit sop (bread soaked in rabbit gravy), bread and milk with a little sugar, and mashed vegetables and gravy, which he called Sunday mush. 'Items like tinned salmon are good enough in emergencies... but a healthy, well-fed cat will seldom eat tinned stuff a second day,' he said.

Cats couldn't wait for their rations from the cats' meat man.

THE CATS' MEAT MAN

When canned cat food was first introduced it was generally believed that cats wouldn't touch it, which perhaps isn't so surprising considering the wide variety of food they would otherwise be given. Today in the United Kingdom only two per cent of owners feed their cats entirely on home-prepared food. The first tinned foods given to cats weren't specifically made for them but were more likely to be tinned pilchards or salmon, which was considered a cheap food. At the time Turner was feeding salmon to his cats it cost just threepence-halfpenny and was enough to last two days.

This compared quite favourably with the two pennyworth of shin, served with broken dog biscuits or hard-baked bread crusts, that was another favourite meal with cat owners. Cats' meat, bought from the cats' meat man, cost about a penny a day but was sometimes so bad it couldn't be eaten. Owners were advised to inspect the meat carefully to see if it was tainted by flies. Initial preparation included dipping the meat in weak vinegar and water, or in boiling water, and rubbing it with a cloth to get rid of any maggots.

The cats' meat man was a familiar sight in the years before the Second World War. He would tour the streets with his gaily painted cart, selling horsemeat and other meats, including trimmings, which were mostly considered unfit for human consumption and sometimes dyed a hideous blue-green colour. The carts themselves were said to be magnificent.

As soon as the tradesman pulled up in his long coat and apron, with his big wicker basket over his arm, hundreds of cats would swarm out of gardens, alleys, trees and byways to greet him. The basket held meat spiked on wooden skewers of different sizes according to their cost. A halfpenny would buy a snack while threepence would purchase a feast. It was said the best customers of the cats' meat man were the humble workers of London who, no matter how hard up they were, wouldn't let their cats go hungry.

The cats' meat man disappeared from the streets of Britain during the Second World War when all meat was rationed. There was little enough for humans, let alone cats. The ration for every man, woman and child in the country was a mere 4 oz (100 g) a week each, so there was little to spare for pets. The small supply of prepared tinned and packet cat foods dwindled, not to reappear until long after the war was over.

FOOD DURING WARTIME

During the First World War, a typical menu was that recommended by a member of the Cats Protection League (CPL). Twice a day she fed her cats bread soaked in milk. She then poured off any excess milk, mixed a small quantity of yeast extract in water, and sprinkled a teaspoon or two of this liquid over the soaked bread. She said her cats were 'plump and splendidly healthy' on this diet.

An 1883 illustration.

The Cat's-Meat Man

HE calls "Meat, meat!"
All down the street;
And dogs "bow-wow,"
And cats "mi-ow,"
While kittens sly
Come purring by,
As if to say—
"Do serve us, pray,
The first of all,
For we're so small."
The man throws bits
Of meat to kits,
And cats, and dogs;
Then on he jogs,
And down the street
Still cries "Meat, meat!"

PURVEYOR OF
CAT'S MEAT
TO HER MAJESTY

At the same time, Mrs Jessey Wade, cat expert and editor of *The Cat* magazine, was recommending 'A good solid pudding as a substitute for meat could be made when convenient. Take any table scraps — bread, potatoes, vegetables and cheese. Moisten with Marmite (yeast extract) liquid, mash well together and put in a pie-dish and bake for about an hour. This, when cold, should be a firm slab, from which slices can be cut, thus making a savoury meal for several days.'

Some experts recommended that a stockpot should be kept going containing plenty of water and any leftover meat. It could be left simmering on the back of the range. A rabbit could be added when available, as well as bones for flavour, plus pearl barley, rice, haricot beans and lentils. The stock would be brought to the boil for a few minutes every day and a little poured over well-toasted leftover bread. It was said that 'Provided stock is not over-diluted, an occasional bowl of liquid will serve as a meal.' Some of the meat and scraps in these stockpots must have been weeks or months old.

There was great concern in 1941 when milk was rationed. However, the Minister of Food announced that cats engaged in work of national importance were to receive an allowance of powdered milk. To qualify, the cats had to be employed in keeping down rats and mice in warehouses where at least 250 tons of food were stored. Their milk allowance was often damaged and unfit for human consumption, which led to the following rhyme which appeared in *Food* magazine:

Pussy cat, pussy cat, where have you been?
I've been for my milk to the pussy's canteen.
But all they could offer a ravenous cat.
Was milk made of powder – and damaged
    at that.

There had been a previous scare for cat-owners in 1940 when the Ministry of Food declared that in future it would be a punishable offence 'to waste food by giving it to pets'. After a public outcry, the Ministry were quick to explain that they meant prosecutions would be confined to cases where human food was used wastefully.

After the Second World War, meat was still in short supply and couldn't be wasted on pets. The austerity years meant owners had to be ever more inventive, so cats began to be fed whale-meat, preferably kept in the water in which it was boiled as it would stay fresher longer and retain its flavour better.

One suggested diet was cooked horse-meat or whalemeat with brown bread and broth, or with green vegetables or raw grated carrots. The evening meal was bread with gravy, or fried bread cubes or baked crusts. Once a week, if it happened to be obtainable, white fish was added.

Certainly, cats of the 1940s ate many more vegetables than today's felines, and leeks and carrots seem to have been favourites. One cat even ate sandwiches of lettuce and grass seed!

ONE **TIBS** A DAY KEEPS THEM FIT AND GAY

MODERN PET FOOD

These were the last days when owners had to worry about their cats' nutrition, how to cook their meals or how to economize on cat food, for by the 1950s prepared food was becoming commonplace.

It all started with an American, James Spratt from Cincinnati, Ohio, who sailed to London to sell – of all things – lightning conductors. When the ship docked, the sailors threw their old, stale ships' biscuits on to the quay, where they were gobbled up by the local strays. This set James Spratt to thinking about producing biscuits specifically for dogs. By the early 1930s he was selling not only dog, bird, fish and foal food, as well as ships' biscuits for human consumption, but had also branched out into prepared cat food, sold in packets at a penny-halfpenny or 7 lb (2.8 kg) bags for three shillings.

Canned foods were literally a different kettle of fish. When Kit-E-Kat first appeared on the market in the late 1930s (only to disappear again during the war), it was treated with suspicion by both owners and cats. Most of those who tried canned food said their cats

44

'wouldn't look at it'. Canned foods were not in common use for humans so there was some consumer resistance at first, but by 1949 a cat shelter worker said that 75 per cent of her charges would readily eat canned food.

Wartime meat rations boosted sales of prepared cat foods. A Kit-E-Kat advertisement in 1939 showed a cat saying 'Keep all your rations and give me Kit-E-Kat.' Within a few years, prepared foods had disappeared from the shelves, victims themselves of rationing. It was the late 1940s before prepared cat food was readily available again and another decade before it was in common use. Now it's the second largest grocery item on supermarket shelves.

Back in 1937, however, canned cat food was so unfamiliar that at least one

I'm doing fine on SPRATT'S CAT FOOD— are you?

Thanks to persistent publicity and the repeated recommendations of satisfied users, Spratt's Cat Food is now the order of the day amongst British Cat owners.

Tell your customers how easy Spratt's Cat Food is to serve—how well it keeps—and how it does away with messy meals. You'll be doing them a really good turn and at the same time you'll be paving the way to a new and profitable market.

Remember Spratt's Cat Food on your counter means **extra** profit in your pocket.

SPRATT'S CAT FOOD

young person made a sandwich with a few tomatoes and some of the meat roll in the larder – it turned out to be the cat's dinner. The verdict? Delicious – just like ham and pork roll.

CAT CARE THEN AND NOW

A FIRM BELIEF held throughout history and still current today runs that cats in previous times were healthier and lived longer. From Victorian days through the 1920s and 1930s, cat-lovers lamented that their cats' average 12 to 14 years of life compared poorly to longer spans in earlier times. In the early 1940s, especially, it was believed that cats were deteriorating because of bad food, inbreeding and kittens being given away too young. In fact, today the average lifespan for a cat is still between 12 and 14 years and owners still complain that cats in previous times lived longer. In 1895, the longest lived cat was 24, much the same age as the longest lived cat in the 1930s and 1940s. The oldest cat ever lived to the age of 35 and died during the 1950s.

By the beginning of this century, veterinary knowledge had improved beyond the old remedies which dictated the eating of a kipper, bones and all, to scour out the insides of a constipated cat, or the swallowing of crushed clay pipes by a cat with the opposite problem.

Just as the early medical practitioners had started in another trade and earned their livings as barbers, so the earliest veterinary surgeons had had a different, but to some extent complementary, trade: they had been blacksmiths and farriers.

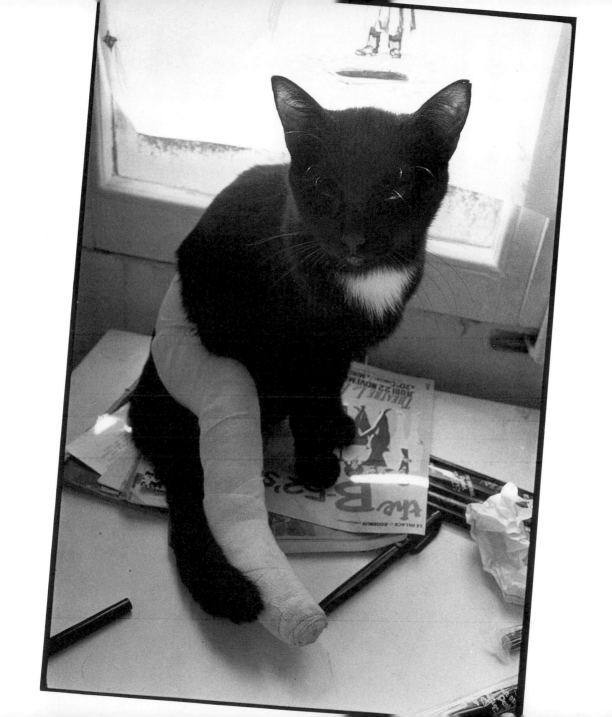

A FEW HOME REMEDIES

As a result it isn't surprising that knowledge of cat ailments was somewhat sketchy at the turn of the century. So much so that 'Two Friends of the Race' (there was a passion for anonymity when writing books at the time) who wrote *How To Keep Your Cat In Health* in 1901 gave remedies only for colds, pleurisy, distemper, mange, worms, fits and those old 'favourites' known to all cat-lovers, diarrhoea and constipation. The 'Two Friends' warned 'If your cat should be taken ill, have as little as possible to do with drugs, unless it be in the homeopathic form'.

The 'Two Friends' suggested that cats with a cold should be given tincture of arsenicum in a spoonful of milk. This potent treatment could also be given for distemper, among other ailments, along with a mixture of eggs, cream and brandy. It could be given for mange, with an external application of sulphur ointment, carbolic acid ointment, green iodide of mercury ointment and 'acid sulphurous lotion', all of which sound horribly poisonous.

Much worse potions were being suggested at the time. Arsenic was considered a tonic and antiseptic, prussic acid was given as an anti-spasmodic and pain reliever, and lead was considered to be an astringent and sedative.

Broken bones were treated with brown paper, strips of calico and a glue pot. The crushed paper was soaked in boiling water, squeezed dry and moulded on to the broken limbs, then glued fabric strips were laid on to hold the papier mâché cast in place.

COMBATING DISTEMPER

By far the most serious cat disease was distemper, now called feline infectious enteritis or panleucopaenia. From the fifteenth century onwards there were a number of serious outbreaks which killed many cats in central Europe and Britain. In 1796 there was a considerable outbreak of the disease in England which extended in the same year to the Netherlands and reached the United States in 1803.

According to 'A Veterinary Surgeon' in his book *The Diseases of Dogs and Cats* in 1893, 'Cats did not formerly suffer from distemper when wild in back gardens the noble tabby ran, but since the long-haired varieties have been largely bred, and the meanest-looking cat may give birth to a long-haired kitten through some casual acquaintance, distemper has become quite common, and many lovely kittens succumb to it despite the most careful nursing and attention.' Throughout history, long-haired cats have been accused of spreading disease to which their shorthaired brethren are supposedly less prone. In the 1990s, for want of anything more serious, they are commonly accused of harbouring ringworm.

Distemper was believed to be caused by high temperatures or drought, and it was thought that outbreaks would diminish as the weather cooled. The treatment was probably worse than the illness – castor oil and liquid paraffin mixed together and given a teaspoon at a time to clear bile. A stomach sedative would be prescribed, and every three hours a cat would be dosed with a dessertspoon of white of egg to which ten drops of brandy had been added. Today, antibiotics and tender loving care are believed to be the best remedies for this serious illness.

SOME OLD WIVES' TALES

Cats were expected to be off colour every spring, going off their food and having bad breath and rough, unkempt coats. Owners were urged to treat these symptoms immediately, otherwise the next stage was constipation, diarrhoea (although not at the same time, presumably), watery eyes, running nose and suppurating ears! In stage three, death was said to be likely from nervous exhaustion, heart failure, enteritis, pneumonia or pleurisy. All this pain and grief could be avoided simply by giving daily tablets of cascara, a laxative made from Californian tree bark.

Tomcats were said to have skin trouble in summer, which was cured by a dose of olive oil twice a week. Owners were exhorted to keep their tomcats healthy so they would sire strong kittens. It was thought that if, after kittening, a female had skin trouble it was because she had mated with an out-of-condition tom.

Oil of many sorts seems to have been a universal remedy. An out-of-condition cat was given olive oil mixed with milk, cream and salad oil beaten together or oil from a tin of sardines. Clogging of the bowel was treated with a dessertspoon of olive oil while a pregnant cat was given a teaspoon of olive oil at least twice a week for the last three weeks – presumably to help ease out the kittens. Fried bacon and bacon fat was considered a good substitute for cod liver oil in 'wasting disease'.

Constipation was treated with an enema of water and glycerine, although only the bravest would attempt giving an enema to a cat. Diarrhoea was treated in 1900 by dissolving 1 oz (25 g) of fresh mutton suet in ¼ pint (150 ml) of warm milk. If the cat wouldn't lap it up, a teaspoon of it was given every two hours.

CONTROLLING THE
CAT POPULATION

At the beginning of the century, the neutering of males was described as 'a great barbarity' by many. This isn't entirely surprising. 'A Veterinary Surgeon' in his book of 1893 gave advice on how to carry out the operation without benefit of anaesthetic by rolling up a tomcat in a blanket. He did not recommend the 'Wellington boot' method which involved immobilizing a cat by thrusting it face-down in a Wellington or top-boot and carrying out the operation as quickly as possible. This anonymous vet said 'Anaesthetics, especially in the shape of chloroform and of ether, are frequently advised for operations on cats. Unless absolute immobility of the animal is required for the success of the operation, I do not like the use of anaesthetics. To begin with, even carefully given, they are dangerous. I have found that animals to which I have given an anaesthetic are more afraid of me afterward than those which I have simply had held properly and produced pain upon. The pain they understand as done for their good; the use of the anaesthetic they do not understand.' If chloroform or cocaine was used, there was an extra fee.

Remarkably, the vet goes on to say 'The subject (of this procedure) if young, may be found at play a few minutes afterwards, alike unconscious of his loss and ungrateful for the trouble he has been saved in the future.'

It would probably be impossible to estimate the number of cats euthanized during the 1930s as it was considered an acceptable Do-It-Yourself task. To put down an adult cat, it was recommended that she be given a saucer of milk or some other treat and while she was busy with that a large footbath or belljar should be placed over her. Chloroform-soaked cotton wool would be placed under the rim and after the cat fell asleep, she should be left for at least half an hour. Then she was to be placed face down in a bucket of water for several hours. (Many cats, apparently dead from the administration of chloroform, had

been known to recover.) Then a decent burial was recommended. Earlier, drowning was advocated for adult cats as it was believed that it was quick and painless – one gasp underwater and the brain would, it was said, form carbonic acid which would put the cat to sleep and render it unconscious before death took place.

KILLING FLEAS AND WORMS

Before the discovery of the effective insecticides we know today, lice were deterred by combing a cat's fur with a mixture of vinegar and water. Alternatively, one part sulphur mixed with ten parts train oil was applied all over the fur, or equal quantities of hydrogen peroxide and water were applied – a remedy which had the added disadvantage of turning cats blonde. It was considered shameful to have an infestation of fleas as it was believed they laid their eggs only in dirty places. They were treated with flea powders – the recommended form of application was to pour the powder into a drawstring bag and place the cat inside with its head sticking out, for 15 minutes. Powders used were flowers of sulphur, powdered tobacco or Persian insect powder. In the case of the latter, it was suggested that the cat be placed on a sheet of newspaper, the powder sprinkled over, brushed out and the paper burned as the fleas would not be dead but only temporarily stunned.

Combs and other grooming aids began to appear in the early 1940s, although only the fine-toothed flea combs were in wide use. One owner took her cat to a clinic in 1938 with very badly matted fur. Asked if she hadn't noticed the cat's condition before it got so bad, she said she hadn't, because she never picked it up. Cats were mainly left to groom themselves at this time.

It was only fairly recently that safe, effective wormers appeared. Some of the first vermifuges were extremely harsh and the mortality rate among kittens was very high. In Victorian times, turpentine was given to kill worms. This inevitably led to cystitis (an inflammation of the bladder), which was then treated with hot hip baths, linseed

poultices between the thighs, warm gruel enemas and opiates. At the beginning of this century, experts recommended adding a pinch of salt to a cat's every meal to prevent worms. An advertisement in 1901 claimed that regular doses of cod liver oil were an excellent antidote to worms.

OTHER AILMENTS

Just as fainting young ladies had bottles of smelling salts waved under their noses, so too did cats when they had fits. Feeding raw meat was thought to be the cause – or taking away all of a mother cat's kittens at one time, which was believed best treated by a warm bath and an enema, as if the poor cat had not already suffered enough! Another theory was a female cat would never have a fit after producing a litter. Cats having fits sometimes had their ears slit and a few drops of blood expelled as a cure.

Apoplexy was considered rare, except in obese cats. The treatment was to clip the fur in two or three places and apply leeches to the resulting bald spots. Extreme cases of dropsy were treated by 'tapping' – removing fluid, bandaging the affected area and then administering brandy in warm milk as a stimulant.

Ulcers of the mouth or tongue were thought to indicate 'internal derangement' and treated with Milk of Magnesia, but pity the poor cat with a sore throat. Until the late 1930s cats were thought to be carriers of diphtheria and so a cat with a sore throat was often euthanized.

A genuine health concern was tuberculosis, or consumption as it was then called. The cause was drinking tubercular milk or eating uncooked meat from infected animals. There was no cure so a tubercular cat was almost always killed.

CAT CARE

Early this century, cat care was basic, even for the pet cat. Few had indoor litter trays, which were then shallow tins or boxes containing ashes, cinders, sand, earth, peat or some mysterious substance called Japanese mould (presumably some sort of moss). Before purpose-made plastic litter trays were available, owners were told to use pans meant for roasting meat, frying pans with the handle removed, or large earthenware saucers from flower pots.

It wasn't until 1947 that the father of cat litter, Ed Lowe, invented a whole new industry and made life much more comfortable for the average cat. Just out of the Navy, with a family to support, Ed was working for his father when a neighbour complained that her cat tracked cat-box ashes all over the house. Ed's father sold Fullers' earth, a natural mineral clay used then as a grease and oil

A modern feline nutritionist and his charges.

absorbent in garages and for nesting materials in chicken farms. It had been used for thousands of years by fullers, who used it to absorb oil from wool, and it had even been used as far back as ancient Roman times as a beautifying face-pack. Ed found a new use for it and a multi-million dollar business was born. His neighbour tried it as a cat litter medium, loved it, and told her friends. Ed went on the road, visiting cat shows, pet stores, grocers and supermarkets, yet it was twenty years before the product really took off. Even today in the United Kingdom, only one third of cat owners provide their cats with a litter tray.

Scratching posts were unheard of and it was recommended that strong brown corrugated cardboard or pieces of rough wood be left on the floor for the cat to strop. Toys were basic too – real rabbits' feet were considered the best playthings. Rather snobbishly, toy mice stuffed with catnip were considered inferior to those without benefit of this herb.

NEW DEVELOPMENTS IN CAT WELFARE

Nowadays the death toll through illness is dropping as more is learned about feline health and new vaccines come on to the market. Feline leukaemia virus (FeLV) was not discovered until 1964 – it is this illness which has been called the cats' Aids, as it depresses the immune system in the same way as the Aids virus. (FeLV is not transmissible to humans.) A vaccine was developed in 1985 in the United States but was not made available in the United Kingdom for fear of possible side-effects. It was not until the beginning of 1992, when an estimated 600,000 cats were suffering from FeLV in the United Kingdom, that a new, genetically-engineered vaccine became available.

The first effective vaccine against feline rhinotracheitis was developed in 1974 and two years later a combined vaccine against rhinotracheitis and calicivirus (often incorrectly called cat 'flu) became available. These viruses were killers (and still are for unvaccinated cats), with epidemics occurring as late as 1978.

It was the 1980s before dietary changes lessened the incidence of feline urological syndrome (the formation of stones in the bladder), which had been considered the most common cause of death the decade earlier. In the mid-1980s, the importance of taurine was discovered and its levels in cat food were adjusted where necessary.

All this research meant healthier cats and less death or destruction for sick ones. Even pneumonia, now easily treated with antibiotics, was fatal at one time. In the 1930s, a New York cat was dying of pneumonia so its owner placed it in a locked garage between the exhausts of two cars with their engines running, believing this to be a humane method of killing it. Half an hour later the owner checked on the cat and to her surprise it stood up, stretched and walked out of the garage, apparently not only unaffected by the carbon monoxide from the exhausts but also completely recovered from its illness.

CATS IN WARTIME

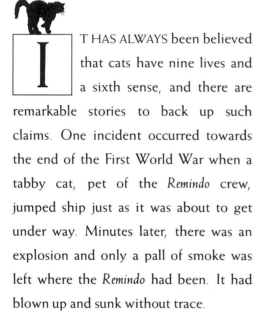

IT HAS ALWAYS been believed that cats have nine lives and a sixth sense, and there are remarkable stories to back up such claims. One incident occurred towards the end of the First World War when a tabby cat, pet of the *Remindo* crew, jumped ship just as it was about to get under way. Minutes later, there was an explosion and only a pall of smoke was left where the *Remindo* had been. It had blown up and sunk without trace.

Tara, a black cat, didn't escape so easily. He jumped overboard in Malta and swam for the shore. The kindly captain sent a boat after him and Tara was brought back, dripping wet. For his own safety, he was placed in a hen coop on the deck until the ship was well out to sea. Several days later, the ship was torpedoed and sank within eight minutes. Tara was one of the crew members who was lost.

One of the happiest endings also took place during the First World War. British troops retreating through Belgium in 1914 found a cat hiding in a farmhouse near St Quentin. Adopted by a soldier, Mons (as he was called) went through six heavy engagements with his new owner. After the war, Mons was taken to Forfar

NARPAC's David Wileman was awarded a bronze medal for rescuing a terrier from a bombed house. He also rescued many other dogs, cats and chickens.

in Scotland (presumably the home of his new owner) and was in constant demand as the star attraction at Red Cross sales where he helped raise £3,000 before his death in 1924.

AIR RAID PRECAUTIONS

By 1938, fears were growing in Europe about the safety of pets during air raids by the German Luftwaffe. The June 1938 issue of *The Cat* advised its readers: 'It would be necessary to put them (cats) to sleep if air raids began, to save them from mutilation and pain; we suggest that cat owners should make up their minds now, while there is no danger, so that there would be no hesitation or loss of time if the danger were to materialize.'

It was realized that pets would not be allowed in public air raid shelters but, in fact, it was another 15 months before the United Kingdom had its first air raid. As the months passed, alternatives other than euthanasia presented themselves. Just as many thousands of British children were evacuated from the cities to the countryside for their safety, so those cat owners who could arrange it sent their cats out of the danger zones. For those with friends in the country-side, this was not too difficult; others had to find boarding catteries. It was inevitable that some cattery owners took advantage and there were reports of overcrowding and cats being shut up in darkness from dawn to dusk. Even where conditions were better, many cats moped and refused to eat.

In Britain, compulsory immediate evacuation took place in some areas but no pets were allowed on transport provided by the authorities. It was suggested that those who had to flee their homes without notice should leave a day's food and water for their pets and inform the police or local animal welfare organizations that an animal was living there. Sadly, these pets often had to be euthanized.

With so many cats being removed from the cities, the numbers of rats and mice reached plague proportions. In Lincolnshire, a campaign was carried out against rats and a cat belonging to a child evacuee was the winner, killing 1,920 rats and earning its owner £16.

As the months passed, and the feared air raids did not take place, the initial panic subsided and suggestions were made for emergency precautions. It was believed that mustard gas and other blister gases would be used against the civilian population (they never were) and every person in the United Kingdom was provided with a gas mask. Gas masks were also invented for animals by a French scientist, but not until the end of 1939. In the meantime, National Air Raid Precautions for Animals (NARPAC) was set up and advice was given on building a gas-proof kennel.

A large wooden box (for example, a tea chest) was to have the cracks stopped up by pasting paper or a waterproof fabric over them. A wooden frame with a mesh centre was the lid. In a gas attack the lid and sides were to be covered with a thin blanket wrung out in cold water. Fortunately, this flimsy contraption was never put to the test.

Bob Martin, who made conditioners for pets, brought out a little booklet in 1939 called 'How to Care for Your Dog and Cat in Wartime'. It suggested that, as protection against blast and splinters, the kennel should be placed in a trench dug in the ground. For gas burns, the affected parts should be scrubbed and covered with a protective ointment made from two parts bleach powder and one part petroleum jelly.

One London owner, obviously unaware that she could make a shelter for her cat herself, telephoned the Lord Mayor of St Pancras at his home in the middle of the night demanding an air raid shelter for her cat. Another handed her gas mask back to her local ARP warden saying she wouldn't be able to wear it as her cat went wild whenever she put it on. 'The gas will just have to poison me,' she said, 'because I won't have Tibby upset'.

While many city dwellers had to use public air raid shelters which prohibited pets, those with gardens could build small private shelters. They were able to take their cats with them when the siren went off – if the cats could be found. One London family who hadn't been able to find their cat left their shelter after the 'all clear' to discover their cat's tail lying in the garden. The young daughter of the house burst into tears at this evidence of the loss of her pet. Next day, the cat turned up for breakfast, bright and breezy but minus his tail.

Scrumpy served in Korea alongside the US Navy.

Some cats came to look on air raids as an adventure. Two Siamese, Suli and Meru, would wait expectantly by their collars and leads when the siren went off. They would prance down the garden and settle down to sleep in their gas-proof boxes. A London cat, without a shelter of its own, would jump on the roof of the public shelter as soon as the siren sounded and cuff any other cat which tried to take over his territory.

Various sedatives were recommended for cats during air raids but many seemed to cause problems. Bromide was often used, but frequent doses caused depression. Other sedatives, such as luminal and chloretone, were only available as tablets which were too big to get down a cat's throat. The favourite sedative was common aspirin – now generally accep-

ted to be toxic to cats. It is not recorded how many more cats died from the result of these sedatives than from the bombs.

FELINE AIR RAID WARNINGS

By 1944, Hitler's scientists had come up with the V-1 – a 12 ft (3.65 m) long pilotless flying bomb, also called a Doodlebug – which carried 100 lb (40 kg) of high explosive. These bombs flew over the British countryside, making their distinctive thunderous racket, until a pre-set mechanical counter cut the engine into silence. The flying bomb would then tip into a dive – with disastrous consequences for those underneath.

Even during the 1967 Six Day War in the Middle East, cats were part of the action.

Most cats quickly learned that air raid sirens meant noise and disruption and learned to fear them. However, many cats didn't need an air raid warning — rather, they became four-legged air raid warnings for their families.

One of the unsung heroes of the Second World War was Billy, a green-eyed blue cat who lived with his owners in Surrey — directly on the flight path of the German aeroplanes on their way to bomb London. Billy quickly learned to distinguish between the noise made by a V-1 and that of an ordinary aircraft. His owners lived in an old farmhouse and kept a large steel chest in the dining room fireplace. If Billy heard a flying bomb, he would scurry to the space between the chest and the back of the fireplace — the safest place in the house.

Of course, Billy's keen hearing far outweighed his owners' and he would dash to his hiding-place long before the family could hear the approaching bomb, so he became a reliable early warning system. By observing their cat, the family knew when it was safe to watch the flying menace and when they should take shelter. About 7,500 flying bombs flew over Surrey in just a few months and Billy gave his family a four-minute warning of every one.

Many cats gave their owners warning of flying bombs in this way. One was a Manx cat which would disappear under a stone staircase — again, the most secure place in the house — well before the sirens went off. As the bombs flew at about 500 mph (800 kph), his owner estimated that the cat could hear them when they were 50 miles (80 km) away.

Was it a sixth sense which made dozens of cats flock out of Exeter in Devon one evening in May 1942? An eye-witness described it as 'an unbelievable exodus of cats' and wondered why they were leaving the city. The reason became clear that same night – a bombing raid devastated the city, killing and injuring thousands of people.

BRAVE SURVIVORS OF THE BOMBS

In 1944, when the flying menace first began, a tabby cat called Tommy hadn't yet learned to associate them with danger. Tommy had been adopted by a London solicitor who fed him fish and milk – he would climb through the window to get it. One day, a flying bomb fell on the building opposite, breaking the windows of the solicitor's office. Tommy leapt out of the window and wasn't seen for four years. The broken windows were boarded up and the boards were not removed until January 1948. Three days later, Tommy reappeared and demanded his lunch.

The home of Snowy, a cat from Ashford, Kent, was completely flattened by a bomb but he lived on the rubble for four years. He refused to have anything to do with any of the neighbours, and appeared to believe that his mistress would return. To make his lonely vigil more comfortable, the neighbours built him a kennel and fed him twice a day.

Many cats were bombed out of their homes and some quickly attached themselves to their rescuers. During the

London Blitz, a cat followed a man to his home in Essex. He let her stay and over the years she had 16 kittens, none of which he would part with. He gave the cats two rooms of their own, despite protests from his mother.

A woman in the south west of England risked death to feed her cat. She had been forbidden to return to her home because of an unexploded bomb but didn't want her cat to go hungry. When she was refused permission by a War Reserve Constable to re-enter the house she sneaked through the barrier. The constable had decided to feed the cat himself and saw her; she was fined £1.

A MEDAL-WINNING CAT

The feline sixth sense led to one wartime cat winning a medal for bravery, the

A war orphan cuddles her cat amid the devastation of the Russian Front.

only civilian cat to do so. Faith was a pretty tabby and white cat who lived in the rectory of the church of St Augustine and St Faith in the shadow of St Paul's Cathedral – an area of London that suffered heavy German bombing raids.

In September 1940, Faith became the mother of a black and white kitten who was called Panda. Soon after his birth, Faith seemed restless and worried. She took Panda out of his basket and carried him down to the basement of the building where she made a bed for him in a recess in the wall. Faith and Panda stayed there and a couple of days later there was a direct hit on the rectory. The following day, without much hope, the rector returned to search for Faith and her kitten. Under some rubble he found the recess... still containing Faith, who had shielded her kitten with her body throughout the long, terrifying night. She received a certificate from the People's Dispensary for Sick Animals of the Poor for 'steadfast courage in the Battle of Britain' and a certificate of honour from the Greenwich Village Humane League of New York.

Faith wasn't eligible for the Dickin Medal, which was only awarded for bravery to animals serving in the Armed Forces, so a special silver medal was struck and presented to her in 1945. Faith's photograph and certificates are still displayed in the tower of the church.

CATS IN OCCUPIED COUNTRIES
Invasion was a fear in Britain but a harsh reality in the rest of Europe. A British

woman living in France in 1940 refused to flee when the Germans arrived because she didn't want to leave behind her three cats and Britain's quarantine laws made it difficult for her to take them into the country. She was interned and spent four years in a camp – all for the sake of her cats, who lived with her friends while she was away.

Five thousand abandoned cats were found on the streets of Paris after just one month of war and thousands more were still roaming around. After the government urged everyone to leave Paris, the cat-lovers who stayed took in as many as five cats each.

In occupied France, cats were sometimes used as couriers. A one-eyed ships' cat named Nelson was rescued from her sinking ship by the French Resistance, then became a member of the underground movement herself. Wearing a disc on a collar containing messages for her rescuer, she would deliver them to him in his hiding places in the French countryside while the Gestapo hunted for him. She survived the war years and lived out her days on her rescuer's farm.

Mourka was a Russian cat who carried messages to HQ from his adopted home in the thick of the Battle of Stalingrad. Used only when it was too dangerous for humans to make the journey, he travelled backwards and forwards for many months. It is thought that he did not survive the end of the battle.

Pets were even found in at least one concentration camp. Many of the internees kept dogs and cats (left behind by villagers who had been displaced to make way for the camp) and shared their meagre rations with them. In the spring of 1943, the Kommandant announced that all pets would be destroyed the following morning. Two months later, something looking like a bag of bones was spotted underneath a bush – it was a thin and starving pregnant cat. She was hidden and, three days later, gave birth to three kittens. There was a ginger who was named Carrots, a grey kitten called Bluebell and Miss Pussy, a pretty tabby. Although the mother cat disappeared when her kittens were weaned, the three survived until, and beyond, liberation of the camp on 12 September 1944.

BRAVERY AT SEA
Ships' cats were much in evidence during the Second World War and some became well-known celebrities. Scouse, the ships' cat of HMS *Exeter* was so famous that he had two portraits painted. He had come through the bombardment of the *Graf Spee* unscathed and became so famous that he was kidnapped in Plymouth; a search party from the ship rescued him. Unfortunately, portraiture seems to have been more stressful to Scouse than bombardment or kidnapping, for he died while being painted. One portrait was presented to his ship and the other was sold on behalf of dependants of the men killed in the Battle of the Plate.

The proverbial nine lives seem to have been owned by Oscar, ships' cat of the German battleship, *Bismarck*. He came to be known as Unlucky Oscar when the ship was sunk under him. Adrift on a piece of timber, he was picked up by the destroyer *Cossack*, which also sank, and he ended up on the aircraft carrier *Ark Royal* – which was sunk as well! Oscar was rescued yet again by the *Ark Royal's* crew, who risked their lives for him. The Dumb Friend's League gave their highest award, a silver medal, to the next ship to bear the name *Ark Royal*. Oscar was put ashore at the Harbourmaster's Office in Gibraltar, and died in 1955 at The Home for Sailors, Belfast, where he had spent his retirement.

The only cat to win the Dickin Medal, given by the Awards Committee of the People's Dispensary for Sick Animals Allied Forces War Cat Club, was Simon, ships' cat of the frigate HMS *Amethyst*. He was given to the ship as a rat-catcher

Simon and the crew of the Amethyst *with a celebratory pie after their daring escape from the Yangtse.*

in 1948. A year later the Red Chinese Army captured the area below Nanking and the *Amethyst* was sent to protect British citizens living there. She ran aground while under fire and many of the crew were injured or killed. Simon was among the wounded, yet he con-

tinued with his job of rat-catcher – the rats would have made an already difficult situation insupportable for the crew. The captain was among the dead so his second-in-command decided to make a run for it down the Yangtse river. They arrived safely in Hong Kong two days later and the remaining crew – including Simon – became heroes.

A triumphal reception was planned for Simon's return home, and a piece of the Dickin Medal ribbon was sent to him to wear before he received the medal. Sadly, he didn't live that long and died in quarantine, having never fully recovered from his battle scars. His medal was presented to him posthumously for 'meritorious and distinguished service', and forms his epitaph, along with this rhyme written in 1949 before his death:

Now here's Simon
For me to make a rhyme on,
Gallant little Simon,
The Amethyst's cat.
Proper Royal Navy!
Give him all the gravy,
He's not daunted
By the stoutest rat.

It's a fitting tribute to all heroic cats.

CURIOUS CATS

THROUGHOUT HISTORY there have been many cases of curious cats. Some oddities, such as cats with dwarfed legs or cats without hair, have surfaced only to die out, then reappear later and become an established breed, such as the Munchkin or the Mexican Hairless cat. Other curiosities appear from time to time only to disappear from public consciousness until the next time one of them is born.

WINGED CATS

Such has been the fate of the curious cats which must be a bird's worst nightmare – cats with wings. In 1897, the first recorded winged feline was discovered in Matlock, Derbyshire and described in a local newspaper as 'an extraordinary large tortoiseshell tom cat with fully grown pheasant's wings projecting from each side of its fourth ribs . . . Never has its like been seen before, and eyewitnesses state that, when running, the animal uses its wings, outstretched, to help it over the ground which it covered at a tremendous pace.' Not only would this cat have been unique because of its 'pheasant's wings' but male tortoiseshell cats are extremely rare.

Whatever the wings were made of, some credulous observers would like us

A winged cat discovered in 1899 in Somerset.

to believe that cats can fly. In 1933, a winged black and white cat was seen in a garden in Oxford. A Mrs Hughes Griffiths found the cat in her stables and saw it jump on to a beam. She described the distance as 'considerable' but apparently did not think of measuring it. 'I do not think it could have leaped – (it was) using its wings in a manner similar to a bird,' she said. The cat was captured and exhibited at a local zoo. Its wings were 6 in (15 cm) long.

The Munchkin, see page 116.

A winged cat which was shot and killed in Northern Sweden was said to have hindquarters covered in feathers, although an earlier report from Professor Rendahl of the State Museum of Natural History made no mention of this, saying merely that the wings were a deformity of the skin which happened to take the shape of wings. The 20 lb (8 kg) cat was 24 in (60.9 cm) long and had a 'wing-span' of 23 in (58.4 cm).

In 1936, a winged cat was found on a Scottish farm near Portpatrick, Wigtownshire. It must have been the oddest-looking cat of all for it was described as being white with long hair, one blue and one red eye, and flaps 6 in (15 cm) long and 3 in (7.5 cm) wide on its back. The wings were said to rise when the cat ran and 'fold down into her side' when she rested.

Douglas Shelton, a teenager from

West Virginia, found a cat with wings in 1959. He and his cat became instant celebrities. After a television appearance a local woman claimed the cat and instituted legal proceedings to get her back. But when the cat was produced in court, she was wingless. She had 'shed' her wings two months after Douglas Shelton had found her.

In Canada in 1966, a winged cat said to be swooping down on farm animals was shot dead and buried but was dug up several days later for examination by scientists at Kemptville Agricultural School. Their conclusion was that the cat's wings were nothing more than matted fur. Interestingly, most, if not all, of history's winged cats seem to have been longhaired which leads one to wonder if the phenomena would occur if a brush or comb was regularly employed. The fur-covered wings of some of these cats may have been congenital deformities, possibly vestigial legs, useless for any purpose at all, including flying.

OTHER FELINE ODDITIES

Deformities in cats are not new. Just as there are Siamese twins in the human world, so there are equivalents in the feline world. In the spring of 1946 in Sydney, Australia, a litter of eight kittens was born, five of which were joined together. They died soon after birth. In July 1946 an English cat had six kittens, four of which shared one thickened leg. They were euthanized but the remaining two tabbies in the litter thrived. A two-headed Red Persian kitten was born in

El Paso, Texas, in September 1946. It lived for five days, feeding with one head while its mother washed the other. She was inconsolable at its death. There have been reports of cats with two tails and a Tennessee cat with four ears. A cat in Michigan had five legs, six paws and thirty toes.

Normally cats have eighteen toes, five on each front paw and four on each back paw. Polydactyl cats have more toes than normal. In Victorian times, extra-toed cats were considered very lucky, especially by sailors, which may explain the increased incidence of these cats on the east coast of the United States. A cat called Mickey Mouse from Westlake Village, California, holds the current record for the most toes. He had thirty-two – eight on each paw.

Some claims cannot be so easily checked and some cat-lovers say things which maybe should be taken with a pinch of salt. In the 1950s, a Mrs Pounds from Dorset wrote to her local newspaper: 'My daughter has a pure white longhaired cat nearly twenty-two years old. It has never been ill or sick and never required spiritual or other healing, and is perfectly well. This cat is most unusual in that it sheds its coat every year, starting at the tail. Gradually the whole skin and fur comes right off and underneath a beautiful new fur appears.'

Another unique cat belonged to the Deems family from Florida. Whitey was a starving stray kitten which was taken in and behaved in a perfectly normal manner until he was about six months old. Then he jumped on to the Deems'

bed and said 'Mama, I'm hungry'. When Ruth Deems expressed amazement, Whitey repeated his statement. Mrs Deems didn't mention the conversation to her husband, but several days later he was stroking Whitey and told him jokingly that he was a bad cat. 'I am *not* a bad cat,' Whitey replied.

In their book *Living Wonders*, John Michell and Robert J M Rickard report that Whitey spoke not only to the Deems but also to their neighbours. One neighbour smacked Whitey with a newspaper for fighting with another cat and Whitey told the Deems 'Mama, he hit me!' When asked what he had been hit with, he is said to have replied 'Newspaper'. Another neighbour tried to pick Whitey up, whereupon Whitey said 'You can't catch me' – he was right.

Whitey spoke at least once a day, often in a complaining manner. He could say many phrases, among them 'Why no one love me?', 'I want to go home', 'I want out' and 'I love Mama'.

Whitey was interviewed by several journalists including Suzy Smith of *Fate* magazine. Unfortunately, Whitey had been ill from poisoning just prior to her visit and refused to say a word.

WATER BABIES

Many cat-lovers are convinced that all felines hate water, yet not only is there a breed of pedigree cat, the Turkish Van, which loves nothing more than a daily dip, but there are many stories of other cats which also enjoy the pastime.

Lady Dorothy Hodges from Exmouth, Devon, was swimming from a local beach, having left her 18-month-old Siamese cat, Otis, on the shore. Glancing round, she found him swimming strongly beside her. After that, he frequently accompanied her on her dip. He was said to swim faster and stay in the water longer than the average swimmer and to use his tail as a rudder.

Waterboy, a two-year-old black cat, was taken to the Angell Memorial Hospital to be rehoused. Passing a tubful of water, he leapt out of an attendant's arms and swam around 'like a trained seal'. When his previous owner, from Cambridge, Massachusetts, was contacted, she confirmed that he often jumped out of the family's canoe and swam to shore when on vacation in New Hampshire, hence his name. Appropriately, Waterboy was sent to live at a naval unit and became their mascot.

Those cats swam for recreation but some cats swim through necessity. A Mrs Magowan of Newry, Northern Ireland, gave her cat Ginger to a friend whose house was on the other side of the Clancy River and the Newbury Canal. The first time he was let out of his new home, Ginger swam the canal, had a short rest, then swam the river to his home. Dripping wet, he arrived demanding dinner.

Strange as it may seem, some cats may even go for a swim as a way to attract attention. One lovely longhaired tortoiseshell became annoyed when she had to move house with her owner, as very little attention was being paid to her. Eventually, in desperation, she threw herself into the canal which ran

by the house. She achieved her object, for her busy owner took the day off work and fussed over her most rewardingly.

The owner of a grocery shop in Malaga, Spain, looked out of her window one day to see her tomcat swimming in the Mediterranean with a kitten in his mouth. On reaching the shore he disappeared for a time, then reappeared to jump back into the sea and carry back another kitten. He did this four times. It transpired that a woman further up the beach had tried to destroy her cat's new-born kittens by throwing them in the sea. The tomcat had saved every one and taken them to a widow whose cat had just had two kittens. The four kittens were placed with the other two and the new mum raised all six. It was generally accepted that the tomcat was the father of the kittens which had been thrown in the sea.

ANTI-CAT ATTITUDES

Attitudes towards cats throughout the centuries have veered wildly between venerating them as gods and burning them as the epitome of evil – plus every shade in between. Attitudes have not changed.

One story that belongs firmly in the Edwardian era shows how cheaply the lives of kittens were held by some people. At the time, the fashion was for large hats lavishly trimmed with feathers, but the collection of these feathers was responsible for wiping out many colonies of exotic birds. Becoming alarmed at the diminishing bird numbers, the conservationists of the period suggested an alternative hat decoration – stuffed kittens.

A Sussex man called Potter developed an interest in taxidermy when a teenager in the 1850s and began to display his stuffed creatures in tableaux. They were all very well received, but the most popular of all featured kittens.

Probably no more than three or four weeks old, the kittens in these displays were obtained through his farming family. They were kittens which were euthanized when their numbers expanded too much and then passed on to Mr Potter for his work. He produced a kittens' tea party, with the kittens sitting around a table sipping tea, and a kittens' wedding with a dressed bride and groom. The museum he founded still exhibits these tableaux today in Jamaica Inn, Cornwall, and they attract as much interest as when they first appeared.

In 1935, cat-owners were still carrying out operations on their animals without benefit of veterinary advice. A man and his son from Buckinghamshire were fined a mere 10 shillings for what was described as a case of 'quackery'. They had operated on a cat with a penknife, without anaesthetic, and it had died. In his defence, the man said he had performed many similar operations and did not know what an anaesthetic was.

A year later, cats were described as 'pests' in the British newspaper the *Daily Express* and a contributor boasted of 'scoring over a cat' by catching it in a rat trap. The *Shooting Times* had just published a list of vermin in order of supposed offences. Cats headed the list.

Amazingly enough, cats are still being

dissected in schools in many states in America as part of biology lessons. Cats are the fourth most popular animal for dissection, although Switzerland, Norway and Denmark have banned dissection from their schools below college level, as has New York. California law gives students the right to refuse to dissect animals; in Maine, students are allowed an alternative animal and, in Florida, pupils need not dissect animals if a parent agrees with their wishes.

THE TRADE IN STOLEN CATS

One supplier of cats for dissection in the United States was said to have sold 125,000 of the animals annually and it was suspected that some were stolen. From the turn of this century to today, owners and organizations have believed there is a trade in stolen cats. They point out that numbers of

The cats' wedding – a taxidermy tableau – from Potter's museum.

cats of the same colour go missing in one area at one time. Earlier this century, it was believed that cats were stolen for vivisection and for experimentation by atomic research stations; tomcats were thought to be stolen for cat fighting. It is believed today that some cats are stolen for dog baiting. The charity National Petwatch believes that tens of thousands of British cats are stolen each year for their fur and indeed, there is a market in Europe for cat fur jackets, coats and trimmings. Despite the large reward on offer, no proof has been forthcoming, just as no proof of cat stealing appears to have been found, despite suspicions throughout the century.

Stealing for fur was as major a concern at the turn of the century as it is now.

Advertisements appeared in newspapers offering to buy rabbit pelts and 'any other skins'. The police, then as now, stated that if any proof of the alleged stealing could be furnished, action would be taken. This echoes what is still happening today. It is widely believed that letting your cat out at night increases its risk of being stolen for fur.

CATS AS COMMODITIES

In the 1940s, cats were considered less as creatures with a right to a comfortable and healthy life and more as commodities. It was still the custom to give live black kittens as good luck charms to brides, actresses, aviators, parliamentary candidates, tennis players and so on. It was considered bad luck to decline the gift and irritation was displayed when, during the winter months, kittens were in short supply and not enough were available as good luck charms.

The Second World War meant there was a shortage of stuffed toys in England by 1943, so kittens, puppies and chicks were bought by doting parents instead, with little thought of how they would be cared for when grown. At the time, a pet store proprietor said 'I have never known such a boom in kittens but they must be black and fluffy.'

In 1946, a correspondent to *The Cat* magazine wrote 'Rarely do you walk home through the streets at midnight without at least one homeless kitten dashing out of the gloom to seek your friendship.' At this time, it was still commonplace to drown unwanted kittens and there were many of those.

WORRIES FOR CAT-LOVERS

Concerns among cat-lovers during the 1930s and 1940s were exactly the same as they are today. They were: overpopulation and unwanted cats; cats being left out at night and injured or stolen for their fur; cats being given milk to drink – sometimes as their only food; cruelty; and owners failing to make provision for their cats when they went on holiday or moved house. (Earlier this century it was considered unlucky to take your cat with you when you moved.)

Female cats were rarely spayed except in cases of 'sexual hysteria' – it was considered a hazardous operation. Contraception was left to the owners of tomcats who were recommended to have their cats neutered. In 1937, the Cats Protection League (CPL) humanely

destroyed 1,096 unwanted, stray and sick cats. Ten years later, this figure had increased threefold. Today the figure for the United Kingdom is less than 50,000, although more than 250,000 cats and kittens enter rescue shelters each year.

The Victorian cat piano – when a key was touched, a lever struck a cat causing it to miaow and a 'tune' was produced from the voices of the various cats.

BENEFACTORS AND PROTECTORS OF CATS

Those who tried to do what they could for cats were considered eccentric at best, maybe even slightly mad. In 1938, a member of the CPL said 'I find the championing of cats takes a certain amount of moral courage because with the uninitiated (and their name is legion) there is something mirth-provoking about cats; in these dull and heavy minds they rank with mothers-in-law and sea- sickness and other such screamingly-funny jokes. 'Only the other day at a party I told my hostess about the CPL. She was a dog-lover and received the information with a polite smile and faintly-raised eyebrows, and I felt as if I had been boosting a society for providing ducklings with bathing-suits!'

Similar attitudes surrounded those who wished to leave money to cats in their wills. An Edinburgh woman left £500 for the care of her cat and was roundly criticized. In the 1940s Miss Louise Baier of New York left a $4,000 trust fund to provide two meals a day for her cat, Tommy Tucker. A Liverpool alderman left £18,000 to a cats' home.

RISKING ALL TO SAVE A CAT

The CPL once provided prizes for children who rescued cats from danger. Four-year-old Myrtle Bethell of Coventry was one of those little girls who liked to dress up her cat and push it around in a pram. While doing so, the cat was attacked by a fierce dog. Myrtle bravely fended it off despite the fact that her cat was holding tightly on to her head at the time. She was injured but didn't let go and was rewarded with a doll.

Two brave firemen, Third Officer Frederick H Briggs and Fireman Anthony Silver, were early examples of fire-fighters who have risked life and limb to save a cat. Actually, they were trying to save an elderly infirm man from a blazing flat above a grocer's shop in June 1939. They were feted for saving the old man's cat and presented with medals and certificates from a welfare organization. They received no recognition whatsoever for saving the old man.

Fire-fighters still risk all to save animals. Recently, Darell Staley from Evanston, Wyoming, was killed in a fall after being electrocuted when attempting

to rescue a cat stranded on a power line. His fellow fire-fighters have established a trust fund for Darell's two children.

Before the Berlin wall came down, a West German cat called Putzi fell over it into the eastern sector. His owner tried to climb over to rescue him but was threatened with rifles by the border guards, so he got his children to make a noise to distract the soldiers while he drilled a cat flap in the wall.

Even murderers can love their cats. A German double murderer was allowed out of jail for a day and absconded. The prison governor threatened to put down the man's two cats if he didn't return. He immediately did so, saying he couldn't be so heartless as to let his cats die.

FAMOUS FRIENDS OF FELINES

The American Civil War had great cat-lovers on both sides. On the eve of a big battle, Abraham Lincoln discovered three kittens; their mother had died. He ordered they should be cared for, and was often seen with them on his lap. His opponent, Confederate General Robert E Lee, was equally fond of cats and, after the war, his letters often reported the antics of his felines.

Cats have also been held in high esteem by American presidents, one of whom introduced the Siamese into the country. President Rutherford B Hayes was known to be a cat-lover so, in 1878, the American Ambassador in Bangkok sent him a Siamese called Miss Pussy. She became known as Siam and was adored by all the family. Sadly, she died nine months later and was stuffed, then sent to the Smithsonian Institute.

President Teddy Roosevelt loved cats, especially Slippers, who was one of the White House felines. Once, some distinguished guests had to step around Slippers because she was lying in the middle of the hall and refused to move. Later on, the President removed Slippers in case the servants were cross with him.

Caroline Kennedy, daughter of John F Kennedy, had a cat called Tom Kitten but after only one month he had to be rehomed because of her father's allergy to dogs and cats.

Calvin Coolidge was the greatest Presidential cat-lover of all. Once at a White House banquet the guests didn't know how to behave in the presence of the President, so they copied everything

US President's daughter, Caroline Kennedy, demonstrating how not to carry cats.

he did. All went well until coffee was served. When Mr Coolidge poured half his coffee into his saucer, his guests followed suit. He added milk and sugar to the coffee in the saucer and his guests copied him. Then he placed the saucer on the floor – for his cat.

COSSETED CATS

SEVERAL DOZEN DIFFERENT breeds of cat are recognized today in the United Kingdom – a number that runs into thousands if all the colour variations are taken into account. However, it was very different at the beginning of this century at a London cat show, when there were basically only five different breeds of cat competing.

Two varieties of longhaired cat were shown – the Angora and the Persian – and eleven varieties of shorthaired cat – the Siamese and Manx plus nine colour variations of what was basically a shorthaired domestic cat. Some of these felines were said to have very strange qualities indeed.

'WRETCHED' BLACK AND WHITE

'It tends more than any other cat to become fat and indolent, or ragged and wretched, as the case may be,' wrote R S Huidekoper in his book, *The Cat*, in 1895. He went on to say 'The Black and White cat is affectionate and cleanly, but it is a selfish animal, and is not one for children to play with.'

Miss Frances Simpson, the cat breeder and show judge, was equally scathing. 'The commonest of all cats are Short-Haired Tabbies and Whites or Black and Whites. The markings are sometimes quite grotesque in their distribution. It seems almost a pity to so far encourage these cats as to give classes for them at our Shows.'

THE HUNTING TORTOISESHELL

Huidekoper claimed the gene which causes the white on a cat's markings is responsible for a drastic deterioration in temperament. 'The Tortoiseshell and White... is apt to become lazy when old – the more so the more white there is in its markings. These cats are excessively cleanly, and vain of their white, spending much of their time in keeping themselves clean.' A tortoiseshell without any white 'is one of the best hunters... is a most patient mouser, and is brave to the extreme. It is not over affectionate, and sometimes even sinister and most ill-tempered in its disposition.'

THE ALL-WHITE CAT

The completely white cat was 'of a timid disposition, very fond of petting and cuddling; it is quiet in its manners, delicate in its temperament, and honest in its character. It would much prefer to be fed from the saucer, and from the table while lying on a chair, than go roaming for prey or stealing from the kitchen. White Cats are, however, sometimes excellent mousers, and are especially popular pets with millers, as their colour can scarcely be seen among the sacks of flour. White Cats are often deaf, and sometimes blind, without any appearance of organic change in the eyes.'

THE 'MONSTROUS' MANX

According to Huidekoper, 'The Manx Cat really can be classed as a monstrosity, having been developed probably by the interbreeding of some freak of nature in the form of a cat which inhabited the Isle of Man at an early period. An ordinary cat can easily be rendered tailless if operated on at a young age... especial attention should be paid to see that the absent tail is natural and that there is no scar as evidence of operative interference, or, as such things are called in dog shows, "faking".'

BANDED AND SPOTTED TABBIES

Tabbies were divided into banded and spotted. Their name was said to have been derived from a street in Baghdad celebrated for the manufacture of its watered or moiré silks. When sold in England, this silk was called atabi or – by those who misheard – taffety.

SIAMESE AND PERSIAN

Of the other pedigree cats, the Siamese was thought to be the most difficult to breed and rear in the United Kingdom. The breed had first been seen in 1871 at the Crystal Palace Show where two Siamese were exhibited. These cats may have died as little is known of them thereafter. Then in 1884 Owen Gould imported Pho and Mia, a breeding pair, from Bangkok and gave them to his sister Mrs Veley. Their progeny won first prizes at Crystal Palace in 1885. One year later, Tiam O' Shian was imported from Bangkok with his less-exotically named mate Susan and, by the mid-1930s, fifty per cent of the Siamese cats in the United Kingdom could be traced back to this prolific pair.

'Tabitha', writing in the *Harmsworth*

Magazine in 1903 said 'Siamese cats, with their quaint markings and horrible voices, are beloved by a few and disliked by many, for it is an undoubted fact that you must either love or detest a Siamese puss. It follows you like a dog, insists on being nursed and addresses you constantly in stentorian tones, evidently labouring under the popular delusion that if you shout loud enough at a foreigner, he will understand your language!'

The first Siamese cats came from the hot and humid climate of Siam (now called Thailand) and were thought not to thrive in the cold and damp British weather. Other breeders thought their problem was a tendency to worms. In 1907, Siamese cats were virtually unheard of in the United Kingdom but by the 1930s they were firmly established as the most popular and numerous breed, a position they have held in the shorthaired world ever since.

The most popular longhaired breed, then and now, was the Persian. The Black was particularly favoured as it was considered lucky, with the Blue following close behind.

Although today the Persian is a specific breed of cat with long, dense fur, tufted ears and a short nose, the turn-of-the century Persian was any cat with longish fur. The pedigree cats of that time would not have been accepted as such today; today the definition of 'pedigree' is a cat which has bred true for three generations – its parents, grandparents and great grandparents all look the same as it does.

EARLY CAT SHOWS

The early cat shows were not at all exclusive – in fact, quite the opposite. The breeding and showing of cats has always interested middle and upper class women, and in the early days they wished to spread their gospel among the lower classes to try to persuade them to treat their cats better. Consequently, the earliest shows had classes intended to attract working men's cats. An alternative story says that when the first show was held at Crystal Palace in 1871, not enough cats could be found as exhibits. The cellars at the Crystal Palace were full of stray cats, so workmen were told to round them up. The generous prizes on offer prompted the workmen to enter their own cats for the show as well, and so working men's classes began.

TOP CATS

First prize in these classes could be as much as 30 shillings – in those days a princely sum of money. It was probably this financial aspect rather than anything else that began to elevate the status of the cat to new heights. Show cats therefore became very valuable – proportionately more so than at any time since – with £25 considered a fair price for a longhaired cat (about the yearly wage of a housemaid). Young kittens cost only two to five guineas but, if they had exceptional looks, became worth £20 to £25 by the age of six months. A tabby cat which won a championship show in 1897 was thought to be worth as much as £50 but its owner turned down all offers for it, although another champion cat was sold for £60.

A good cat, shown regularly, would win prizes worth up to £20 a year for five or six years. A cat was considered to be in its prime from the age of five to six; after then it was thought its spine would begin to drop and it would die between the age of eight and nine.

Miss Simpson, as a show judge, said with authority 'Apart from the length and texture of fur, the points of the animals are practically the same, whether long- or short-haired. They should be cobby in build and short on the legs, the head should be round and broad, eyes large and full, nose short, ears small and wide apart.' This suggestion would horrify today's pedigree experts.

HRH Princess Michael of Kent with Magic, one of her Siamese.

SENDING A CAT OFF TO
A SHOW

British cat shows at this time were two-day events, rather than the one-day shows held in the United Kingdom now. Many owners did not trouble to attend. They simply sent their cats off by train and hoped they would arrive safely, be fed once they arrived and, after the show, be sent back without mishap. Of course, this complicated series of events rarely passed off exactly as planned.

The more fortunate cats were put on the train in wicker cat baskets or hampers and it was suggested that, in order to keep out draughts, brown paper should be wrapped around every side of the container except for the handle. Padlocking the container was considered a good idea, in which case the key should be posted to the secretary of the club holding the show. Hopefully, the basket would not go astray or be delayed, in which case the cat might spend several uncomfortable days trapped in its container until it was found.

Owners who did not possess cat baskets used wooden crates, which they nailed down, or margarine baskets, strapped shut. In these cramped containers, without food or toilet facilities, the cats were sent on journeys which were sometimes extremely long. Worse still, some owners sent their cats to shows in sacks tied around the neck so only their heads protruded. Cats with the bad habit of scratching, particularly at their neck ruffs so they would be thin and patchy, had their hind legs tied together with wash leather. The return

journey was no less fraught – some owners never got their own cats back at all. One woman sent a female cat to a show and a male was returned. She didn't notice, and put the male in with her cattery of females – with unexpected results two months later. She had noticed that the cat she got back was particularly heavy, but thought it had just been well-fed at the show.

Unaccompanied cats could be insured with the railways for threepence in the pound. Owners would spend threepence on insurance, believing it ensured better treatment for their felines, whatever their worth. Experts suggested that cats should not be fed before their journey; at a two-day show there was 'hope and trust' that they would be fed when penned. Some criticism was voiced about show managers feeding their charges milk instead of water, with consequent 'accidents' on the day of the show or on the return journey.

VETTING-IN AT A SHOW

Diarrhoea was one of the least of the worries of the early cat shower. An illness called show fever sometimes wiped out entire catteries within a few hours of them returning from a show. Although show fever was probably feline

infectious enteritis, for which there was no preventative inoculation at the time, many owners thought their cats had been poisoned. (Cats are more likely to be poisoned *today* in a British show as there are many petty jealousies between a few breeders which have led to cats having bleach poured into their drinking water, hatpins stuck into their bodies or noxious substances sprinkled on their fur. All this despite the fact that there is little or no immediate financial reward for show wins today, merely a rosette worth a few pence.)

Show fever was the result of little or no inspection from the show vet, called vetting-in. Today all cats are vetted-in to every British show although vetting-in is still not carried out at all shows in the United States. A veterinary surgeon is in attendance at every United Kingdom show, inspecting every cat thoroughly for signs of illness or parasites before it is allowed in. Inoculation certificates are inspected and if a cat appears unwell, it is not allowed to compete in the show.

EXHIBITING THE CATS

Most cats were exhibited in pens, lined with straw, although some had silken

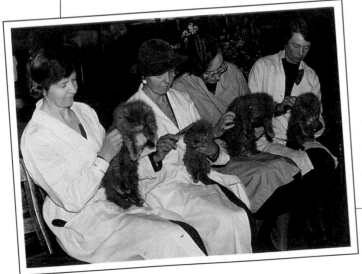

Preparing Persians during a 1937 cat show.

drapes to decorate their pens and velvet cushions on which to recline. Visitors were often kept behind ropes – a sensible precaution which could well be re-introduced today, as disease is so easily transmitted from cat to cat by touch.

Cats today are entered in classes according to their breed and colour, but there were many extra classes at the turn of the century which would not be countenanced now. There were litter classes, where young kittens were dispatched to shows with their mother – and sometimes did not survive the experience. Five good kittens were considered superior to three. There were classes for pairs of kittens, the heaviest cat, and even for deportment. Cats were paraded around the ring on ribbons and given extra points if they and their owner

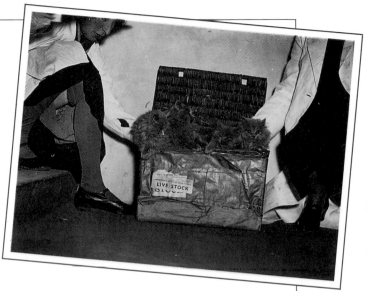

How cats were often sent to shows – in baskets wrapped in brown paper.

looked attractive together and the cat appeared happy to walk on its lead.

Cheating was rife; not only was there the surgical removal of tails to turn ordinary cats into Manx, but dyeing was commonplace. Blue cats were very popular, coming second in popularity only

A cat show of the 1950s.

to black cats, so cats of a nondescript colour were sometimes dipped in dye to turn them into Maltese cats, as they were then called. According to the 1900 edition of *Our Cats* magazine, the dye, which dried almost instantly, did not produce a solid effect and had to be supplemented with dye applied with a comb. The cat's nose, where the hair was short and fine, was dyed using a sponge. Producing a Maltese only took about an hour, whereas a tortoiseshell fake took three hours as the dye had to be applied in patches with a comb.

In 1934, British cat fans called for a French innovation to be introduced into the United Kingdom: French cat shows were holding classes for the 'ratting cats' from shops and stores. The cats were judged entirely on condition, not on

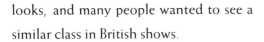

looks, and many people wanted to see a similar class in British shows.

In the same year, a show was held in the United Kingdom which was heralded as the first in which the domestic (i.e. non-pedigree) cat was to be featured prominently and given some special classes of his own. The sole standard was to be good condition and the show was promoted by *The People* newspaper. Sixty domestic cats were entered.

INTEREST IN CAT BREEDING

Needless to say, the interest in cats as show specimens, as well as in the money they were able to earn as prizes, generated an interest in their breeding. It was considered to be a remunerative career, with kittens realizing good prices and stud fees to be gained from good male cats. With top-quality show kittens worth up to £25 at the age of six months, and stud fees in 1900 of between $5 and $10 in the United States and 1 guinea in the United Kingdom, increasing to £2 10 shillings in the 1930s, perhaps it was little wonder that cat breeding was considered to be a cheap hobby that could be turned into a money-making career. Even after the Second World War when kitten prices had dropped (probably as a result of reduced cash prizes in cat shows as well as the general shortage of food), pedigree kittens were selling for between four and six guineas each – several week's wages for a working man.

A lucrative export trade had sprung up between the United Kingdom and the United States, with up to £20 being paid for first-class British kittens. British breeders were even exporting Blue Persians to Persia, as the British ones were more beautiful.

CAT BREEDING OVER THE YEARS
Those wishing to become professional cat breeders were advised to take a job for two years at a cattery to learn the trade. They were told to visit cat shows and meet as many people as possible in the business. Yet they were given some strange advice by the experts.

The cats were usually housed in outdoor catteries, fairly similar to those in use today, with beds made out of barrels or wooden chests and filled with hay in winter and paper in summer. It was suggested the outdoor enclosures should never be heated as that would make the cats susceptible to illness.

Dyspepsia was considered another common failing of pedigree cats. It 'is more often met with in highly-bred and notably show specimens, when a too-fixed and stimulating system of feeding is adopted', according to the 1901 book *How to Keep a Cat in Health*. Horse meat was not given to such highly-bred animals but mutton was, chopped in small pieces with the fat taken off. (The fat would have made the meat more palatable to the cat and would have caused no ill-effects but this wasn't realized then.) Water 'with the chill taken off' was given to drink.

Pedigree mothers, it was said, should not be expected to bring up litters of more than four kittens, and for larger litters a foster mother should be used. Also, if the pedigree queens were not good mothers (an occurrence which, today, would bring forth the suggestion that they should not be used for breeding at all) a foster mother should be found. Foster mothers could be obtained from cats' homes and were unwanted pregnant cats due to kitten at around the same time as the pedigree queen. When the foster mum gave birth, all her kittens except one would be taken away and euthanized, and the pedigree kittens substituted.

It was believed that if a pedigree queen had had a liaison with a mixed-breed cat, her progeny would be tainted for ever more. A Persian who had 'strayed from the path of virtue' was said to have had remarkably poor specimens of kittens from a good sire – 'what might be called half-breeds'. Owners mated their

were often advised to have a blue one as they were less likely 'to show the dirt' and white kittens were not recommended at all for anyone living in a city.

Then, as now, many owners kept one or two queens but no stud, so used a 'public' stud cat when their female was ready for mating. The stud cat usually lived in an outdoor stud house, just as he does today, and the queen in season would visit him. Although today very few owners would let their queens go for mating without taking her themselves, earlier this century they were dispatched in much the same way as show cats, in a basket, together with the stud fee and their return railway fare. Needless to say, when many queens arrived at the breeder's home they had entirely gone off the idea and had to be sent home

female towards the end of her season if they wanted male kittens. It was believed that if the stud cat was fed well, rested and strong, females would predominate in the litter.

In the days when transport was not so easy as today, kittens were often sent 'on approval' to a prospective new owner. If they didn't like them, they were sent back. Those wanting to buy a kitten unmated, so sometimes the stud cat would be dispatched to the queen instead, and the charge would be a fee plus a kitten from the resulting litter.

There was a special class at shows for stud cats; they were not judged themselves but their progeny was. This was an excellent idea as many very good-looking stud cats seem incapable of passing on their good points to their offspring, while some indifferent males have excellent kittens (although mum plays a part too, of course).

It was thought vitally important that the stud be kept busy with plenty of visiting females. A C Jude in *Cats and Kittens* thought a stud would become semi-sterile, producing a high proportion of dead sperm, if not used regularly. He said 'Long periods of disuse are injurious, as an undue accumulation of semen in the generative passages will result in back pressure, which will adversely affect the spermogenetic capacity of the testes and possibly also interfere with the functional activity of the accessory sexual glands.' It was obviously to learn gems like this that breeders studied at a cattery for two years.

At the turn of the century, sexual matters were not discussed with the openness with which they are today and this was true even of cats. So when a young boy asked his mother where their queens went at those regular intervals when they disappeared to stud, he was told they went away 'to learn manners'. Observing the behaviour of one of the queens on their return he said 'Mother, they really do come back better behaved'.

THE CATS OF TODAY

BY THE YEAR 2000, it is estimated that there will be 69 million cats in the United States. It's an increase of around one million per year – and cats, which already outnumber dogs in the United States, will continue to do so throughout the next century. In the United Kingdom, it is expected that the number of cats will increase twice as quickly as dogs and that, after 1995, cats will actually be more numerous. In Japan, there is a cat boom with an increase of more than 20 per cent over five years to a population of more than five million. Already in the Netherlands, Austria, Finland, Norway, Portugal, Spain and Switzerland there are more cats than dogs; a trend which seems set to be followed in many other countries.

THE FELINE TOP TEN

In all countries, there are more mixed-breed cats than any other type. Approximately 93 per cent of cats in the United Kingdom are of mixed ancestry ('moggies', as they are known), while in the United States they number about 60 per cent. Of the pedigree cats it has been said that only two breeds exist – Persians and everything else!

In the United States in 1990, the Cat Fanciers' Association registered almost 85,000 pedigree cats, of which more than 60,000 were Persians. In second place in the United States Top Ten was

the ubiquitous Siamese, while there was a patriotic new entry at number three — the Maine Coon, up six places in twelve years. Places four to ten were taken by the Abyssinian (thought to be a good cat for a man because of its similarity to a cougar), Exotic Shorthair (the lazy person's Persian), Oriental Shorthair (Siamese in another coat), Scottish Fold — a cat not accepted by the British Governing Council of the Cat Fancy (GCCF) because of its 'folded' ears — Burmese, American Shorthair and Birman.

In Europe, to no one's surprise, the Top Ten also shows a slightly patriotic bias. So in Sweden, the number three feline is the Norwegian Forest Cat, accounting for one-seventh of all registrations (which total less than 9,000).

Surprisingly, the Siamese comes fourth, with only one-twenty-eighth of total registrations. The Persian is first (again) with almost half all registrations, the Birman a not-very-close second, then, after the Norwegian Forest Cat and Siamese come the Burmese, British Shorthair, Abyssinian, Russian Blue, Cornish Rex and European Shorthair.

In the United Kingdom, first place goes to the Persian and second to the Siamese, with the British Shorthair in third place. Other longhairs are becoming popular, with Maine Coons and Norwegian Forest Cats rapidly gaining in popularity. The number of pedigree kittens registered each year has increased from an all-time low of 400 in 1940, to 25,000 in the early 1980s and 36,000 in the 1990s.

REX CATS

Not only are the most popular breeds of cat changing, but today the species itself is changing. Increased knowledge of genetics leads to 'sports' (natural mutations which ordinarily would have disappeared within one or two generations) being preserved and their mutated genes passed on to subsequent generations.

Throughout history there must have been many examples of the short and curly-coated cat now called the Rex but it wasn't until the 1940s in East Berlin that the German Rex became established as a breed, and the 1950s and 1960s that curly-coated kittens born to normal-coated cats in Cornwall and Devon led to the establishment of Cornish Rex and Devon Rex.

THE SPHYNX

In the 1830s 'the scant-coated cat of Paraguay' was described by the German naturalist Johann Rudolph Rengger. By the end of the century, the Mexican Hairless cat, as it came to be known, was being exhibited at cat shows in the United States and thirty years later it was declared extinct. During the 1980s the Sphynx, as it was now called, was said to number a mere twenty or so cats throughout the world. Yet by the 1990s, the Sphynx was thriving, especially in the United Kingdom, thanks to out-crossings to Rex cats which strengthened the breed but retained the lack of fur. It is a good example of how knowledge of genetics, cat care, medicine and nutrition can promote a breed which may not have survived in previous times.

THE MUNCHKIN

Another unusual looking cat was described in the 1944 *Veterinary Record*. H E Williams-Jones described four generations of cats which looked more like dachshunds than cats. They had shortening and bowing of the long bones of the leg, which did not appear to hinder their movements or their ability to play. Again, in the 1950s a Russian cat, dubbed the Stalingrad Kangaroo cat, was born with a similar deformity. Just like the Paraguay and Mexican cats, these oddities died out until they reappeared in Louisiana in the 1980s and eventually formed the basis of the breed now called the Munchkin, after the tiny people in the film *The Wizard of Oz* (see the photograph on page 78). Although very few members of this breed are believed to exist, the few that do have caused a furore amongst cat-lovers and registration organizations such as the GCCF which insist that cats with such deformities could never be accepted as a breed.

THE CALIFORNIA SPANGLED CAT

Many new breeds of cat do not come about as a result of a natural mutation but

The magnificent – and rare – Manx.

because of careful breeding over many years. They are just as likely to cause controversy: it would seem that cat-lovers throughout the ages have had fixed ideas on which cat breeds and colours should exist and will not readily accept variations. For example, in the late 1940s there were still breeders offended by the suggestion that the Siamese should be any colour but Seal Point, referring to the new Chocolate Points as mongrels. A more recent example of this resistance to change is the California Spangled cat.

Unleashed on what should have been an enthralled public at Christmas 1986, this beautiful cat caused enormous controversy throughout the cat-loving world. It took 11 generations for its American breeder to produce this spot-

Sphynx kittens – a growing breed.

ted domestic cat with a look of the wild but a playful and affectionate temperament. What may have caused the trouble was the fact that the cats were sold through a department store, even though that store was Neiman-Marcus in Dallas, famous for selling his 'n' her Lear jets as Christmas gifts. Charges were levied (without foundation) that these were designer pets bred to match the wallpaper, although the store took pains to vet prospective owners. The $2,000 price tag probably ensured criticism in some quarters.

TYPICAL CAT OWNERS

According to psychologist Jane Firbank, there are four groups of people most likely to own cats. The first is the couple, married or living together, who are as yet childless but appreciate practising their nurturing skills on their surrogate feline family. How each partner copes with the cat can provide a clue as to how he or she would cope if the couple were to have any children.

The true baby symbols are the long-haired cats, with their large eyes, round faces and cuddly appearance. According to Jane, these cats appeal to people who need people, often those whose livelihood depends on their own appearance, such as celebrities and media folk. They are also popular cats with the wives of successful men. Sleek shorthaired cats appeal to freedom-loving owners with a degree of unconventionality in their make-up. Practical, down-to-earth people, who are not image-conscious, prefer owning mixed-breed cats.

When the American Society for the Prevention of Cruelty to Animals held a drive to rescue New York's stray cats, 348 were picked up in one day.

THE GROWING CAT
POPULATION

Cats continue to increase in numbers because busy families believe cats are less troublesome pets than dogs. They don't need to be taken for walks and they are seen as better apartment-dwellers. In 1975 (as in 1935) there were just under 6 million cats in the United Kingdom and in 1990 the figure reached 6.8 million. According to the welfare organization, Adopt-a-Cat, there are an estimated 250,000 cats and kittens each year which find their way into shelters. Fortunately, much fewer of those are put to sleep than in 1935, when an estimated 250,000 unwanted cats and kittens were euthanized in the United Kingdom.

Too many kittens and not enough good homes has been a constant problem and the population explosion at the beginning of the century was mainly contained by destroying female kittens and strays. At the turn of the century, the London Institution for Cats 'owing to the enormous number of cats daily received, can only keep the best of the strays alive for 24 hours at most; and when diseased or wounded or in overwhelming numbers, the worst of them are mercifully destroyed at once.' Owners of female cats were constantly concerned with finding homes for unwanted kittens because, left to their own devices, queens can have up to five litters a year.

From the turn of the century until the 1930s, spaying was rarely carried out as it was considered dangerous, difficult, inhumane and extremely cruel. When females had kittens, owners were advised to destroy all the kittens except one, to stop the mother fretting. Kittens were to be left with their mother for a few hours while they suckled milk and the owner chose the one that was to survive. A male was recommended, pretty and evenly marked, and the others were to be removed when the mother left her bed. Much irritation ensued when

kittens thought to be male turned out to be female after all. In one shelter, almost every cat destroyed was a female who had been given as a male. In general, twice as many cats were euthanized because they were pregnant than because of illness.

In the February 1935 issue of *The Cat* this advice was given, 'When getting a kitten, choose a male; when he is about six months old, take him to a Veterinary Surgeon or dispensary for a little opera-

tion. This will make him a better house pet, less inclined to stray.

'If your cat is a female, do not keep all her kittens; only one Tom; take the others to a shelter to be put to sleep.'

Figures are not easy to come by, but today in the United Kingdom most of the cat shelters (which number about 400) do not destroy cats unless they are terminally ill. The exception is the Royal Society for the Prevention of Cruelty to Animals (RSPCA), which euthanizes approximately 33,000 cats each year. Most United Kingdom shelters neuter or spay cats before rehousing them or, if they are too young for the operation, extract a promise from adopters that they will have their kittens de-sexed in order to prevent even more unwanted kittens. In some areas of the country, notably the south, as many as 90 per cent of cats are neutered.

In the United States, due to the large cat population (estimated currently at around 60 million) the figures are staggering. According to the American Humane Society, 3,500 kittens are born every hour, compared to only 415 humans. That means 30 million new kittens are born every year. In 1989, almost 6 million cats found their way into America's 3,600 shelters and less than one quarter found new homes. The rest were euthanized. Half the adopters do not return as promised to have their cats de-sexed when they are old enough. Every year in the United States, 15 million cats and dogs are destroyed because there are not enough homes for them.

Shelters do all they can to find homes, including using clever advertising techniques. The Amanda Foundation in Los Angeles places a notice almost daily in the *Los Angeles Times* advertising their unwanted cats as 'Down and Out in Beverley Hills'. Many individuals do what they can to help homeless cats and, realizing how overburdened the shelters are, try to keep as many strays as possible themselves. One woman in Wyoming ended up with 126 cats simply because most of them had nowhere else to go.

Some cats spend most of their lives in shelters – some can live there for 15 years or more. Occasionally this is due to extreme nervousness on the part of the cat, and such cats are considered unsuitable for rehousing. Others may not appeal to prospective adopters because of a disability (a missing eye or paw, for example), although such cats often make wonderfully friendly pets as they seem to appreciate having a home of their own again. Other cats are simply the wrong colour. Blue cats and tortoiseshells, especially longhaired ones, are in great demand but in many places black cats are unpopular and are left behind.

FERAL CATS

It could be said that these shelter cats are the lucky ones; many thousands of unwanted cats are simply turned out to fend for themselves. They revert to the wild, becoming feral and living without human company. Feral cats congregate in groups in areas of human habitation but usually without human contact.

Hospitals and industrial sites are favoured places because they provide some degree of warm air and edible rubbish which can be scavenged. People who live in the area will often feed the cats too and their daily visits come to be expected by the cats, even though they may not approach or show any degree of friendliness. In 1977, it was estimated that there were over 700 colonies of feral cats throughout the United Kingdom.

There is some disagreement over the handling of feral cat colonies. At one time, pest control companies were automatically called in when noise, smell and health hazards such as fleas became overwhelming and they would euthanize entire colonies. In the 1970s and 1980s, welfare organizations started trap-and-neuter policies. The cats would be trapped, taken to a veterinary surgeon who would anaesthetize them, neuter them and cut a tiny piece off the tip of the ear for identification purposes in the future. Once they had recovered, the neutered cats would be taken back to where they had been found.

Although trap-and-neuter policies cut down on the number of kittens born, other organizations believe it is cruel to keep feral cats alive when they are so

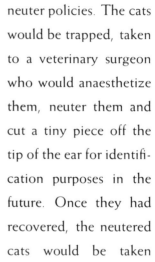

obviously unwanted. In some areas, strong measures are being introduced to prevent unwanted pets being born in the first place. San Mateo County, California, is the first place in the United States to have passed an ordinance which states that cats and dogs must be neutered if their owner does not have a breeding licence. Fines for an infraction of the law start at $100 for a first offence, rising to $500 for subsequent offences.

THE LAP OF LUXURY
Life can be hard for the homeless cat but cats with good homes have never before lived in such luxury and comfort. The pampered pet can be tempted with canned gourmet meals containing lobster, crab or prawn. His owner may have bought him a carved four-poster bed, or a brass bed with a lacy quilt. Indoor cats can be persuaded to exercise on floor-to-ceiling climbing frames, carpeted to match the rest of the decor, or the cat can use his scratching post, specially fitted with a battery-operated toy mouse rotating around the top.

If bored, the cat of today can lounge in front of the television, watching his very own video of birds flying from branch to branch. His personal groomer may visit to give him a deluxe wash and brush up at home. If he is ill, he has access to medical facilities as good as those for humans, and his vet may also be a qualified homeopath and herbalist. Bach flower remedies can be used on him, or crystal healing. If life is getting him down, a behaviourist will investigate his psyche.

He can have his horoscope cast or a song custom-written for him. In cold weather, there are polo-neck sweaters for puss and, in summer, T-shirts bearing appropriate messages. Alternatively, he can wear a leather collar in the shape of a wing collar with a bow tie and 24 carat gold-plated buckle. If he lives in California, he can get married in a ceremony complete with music, confetti and a wedding certificate. In Japan, he can visit a health farm and take up yoga.

It's a life undreamt of by the humble mouse-catcher of the last century. The mouser was made redundant when powerful rodent poisons were developed but now rodents are becoming immune to those poisons. So in years to come, it may be back to work for the pampered puss . . . but that's another cat's tale.

INDEX

ACKNOWLEDGEMENTS

The author would like to thank the following people and organizations for their assistance with research for *Cat Tales*: all the staff at the Cats Protection League headquarters in Horsham; the Governing Council of the Cat Fancy; the Cat Association of Britain; the Cat Fanciers' Association; Brian Doyle and Peter Embling from *Cats* magazine; Alan Walker MRCVS, Geoffrey West MRCVS, Julian Clegg and Amanda Birch from Radio Sussex; Dick Meadows from BBC Norwich; Tony Lawton; Cyril Rogers; Mrs Ella Johnston; Mrs Christine Holford; the Pet Food Manufacturers Association; Hi Life Gourmet Pet Foods; J Salmon Ltd; Miss J A Joubineaux at Her Majesty's Treasury; Miss Allison Derrett of the Royal Archives Windsor Castle; *Cat Fancy* magazine; and the Royal College of Veterinary Surgeons.

PICTURE CREDITS

The author and publishers wish to thank the following for permission to reproduce photographs and illustrations:

Ancient Art and Architecture Collection, p 7; Animal Photography, pp 116, 120, 121, 125; Animals Unlimited, pp 48, 91, 124; Bridgeman Art Library, p 103; British Rail, p 15; Stephe Bruin, p 117; Camera Press, p 93; Henri Cartier-Bresson/Magnum, p 109; Cheltenham Art Gallery/Bridgeman Art Library, p 21; Cornell Capa/Magnum, p 67; Mary Evans Picture Library, pp 9, 16, 41, 70, 89, 95, 97; Fortean Picture Library, p 77; Lesley Fotherby/Chris Beetles Gallery, pp 99, 110; Martine Franck/ Magnum, p 113; Jean Gaumy/Magnum, p 53; Glenturret Whisky Distillery, p 32, 33; Hulton Picture Company, pp 13, 19, 23, 27, 30, 38, 61, 65, 74, 75, 104, 105, 106, 119; David Hurn/Magnum, p 29; Erich Lessing/Magnum, p 10; Loveapet Products, p 126; Peter Marlow/ Magnum, p 55; The Bob Martin Company, p 44; National Magazine Co., p 37; Michael Nichols/Magnum, p 58; Derold Page/Bridgeman Art Library, p 98; Norman Parkinson/Camera Press, p 101; A & F Pears Ltd, p 24; Potters Museum, Jamaica Inn, Cornwall, p 86; Guy Le Querrec/Magnum, p 81; Spillers Foods, p 45; Victoria and Albert Museum/Bridgeman Art Library, p 83; Tetsu Yamasaki/Dr Solveig Pfluger, p 78; Patrick Zachmann/Magnum, p 47;